FOLLOW YOUR DREAM

I dedicate this book to my parents,
my family, my friends,
and my fellow Jesuits
These have taught me
what God's dream for us is like.

I spread my dreams beneath your feet
Tread softly because you tread on my dreams.
W. B. Yeats

PETER HANNAN SJ

Follow Your Dream

RESTORING LOST INTIMACY

THE COLUMBA PRESS
1993

First edition, 1993, published by
THE COLUMBA PRESS
93 The Rise, Mount Merrion, Blackrock, Co Dublin
Cover by Bill Bolger
Origination by The Columba Press
Printed by
Loader Jackson, Arlesey
ISBN 1 85607 063 8

Author's Note

I want to thank Laurence Murphy SJ, Kieran Hanley SJ and all those whose interest and encouragement has meant a lot to me as I laboured to write this book. I would like to thank Genevieve Tobin who has influenced the shape and content of this book in such a profound way. I thank her for her encouragement, her inspiration and for all the time and effort she has put into being such an insightful critic. Three people in particular have influenced the content and method of this book: John Hyde SJ, Bernard Lonergan SJ, and Dr Ira Progoff.

Contents

PART IV

PART V

CHAPTER 1

The dream in the acorn

It is awesome to think that a huge oak tree is the realization of something that was in the acorn from which it grew. We might call what was in the acorn a plan or a *dream*. This was built into it and directed each stage of its growth on its way to becoming a majestic tree. The tree did not grow at random, for even though it was shaped by circumstances such as storms, the main thrust of its growth came from the dream built into it. The tree's growth is always being directed by this plan of God deep within it.

Our lives too are directed by a dream God has built into us, but we differ from the oak tree, in that the fulfilment of our dream is not automatic. We have to get in touch with it and decide to take responsibility for its realisation. It is very easy for this 'still small voice' of God, directing us unerringly, to be drowned out by other concerns. It is vital that we become more familiar with the voice of our dream and let our lives be guided by it.

In this book, I will use this symbol of the dream that lies deep within us, instead of the more traditional term, the will of God. Fully understood, they both mean the same thing. However, the term 'will of God' has often been understood by people as an outer authority, and this outer authority has been trusted to the near exclusion of the inner authority with which God's 'still small voice' speaks. The term 'will of God' is also understood to be mainly concerned with what we do, whereas the idea of the *dream* stresses more the vision and the values that inspire our behaviour.

What kind is our dream?

There are a number of ways of looking at our dream that may help us to develop a sense of the richness of this symbol.

1) Our dream is *innate*, or built into us. It is like the dream which inspires the birds to build their nests in Spring, or which guides

the bulb on its way to becoming a beautiful tulip. Our dream is thus irrepressible and will keep asserting itself and surging up into consciousness, no matter how much we tend to overrule it. Our dream is not just something we long for, but a thirst that we *are*.

I will put my law within them, and I will write it on their hearts; and I will be their God and they will be my people. No longer shall they teach one another, or say to each other, 'Know the Lord', for they will all know me, from the least of them to the greatest. (Jr 31:33-34)

2) The dream in each of us, like that in the acorn, is also *unique*. Just as there will never be another oak tree, like the one that emerges from the dream in a particular acorn, so each of us can say, 'There will never be another me'. This uniqueness is what is referred to in Scripture when it says that God calls us by our name. In the Bible, a name sums up a person's unique relationship with God. The uniqueness of this relationship finds expression in the distinctive way along which each of us is drawn. It is very different from the way along which anyone else is led.

And now this is what the Lord says, he who created you, O Jacob, he who formed you, O Israel: Fear not, for I have redeemed you; I have called you by name, you are mine. (Is 43:1)

3) Another important feature of the dream in the acorn is that it is realised in a very *constant* way, one that is consistent with the unique way the tree has grown so far. Similarly, every step we are drawn to take towards realising our dream, flows very naturally out of what has gone before. This constant way our dream develops, will show in the recurring patterns of enlightenment and attraction which form the ideals and priorities peculiar to each of us.

The Lord your God, who goes before you, is the one who will fight for you, just as he did for you in Egypt before your very eyes, and in the wilderness, where you saw how the Lord your God carried you, just as one carries a child, all the way that you travelled until you reached this place. But in spite of this, you have no trust in the Lord your God, who goes before you on the way to seek out a place for you to camp, in fire by night, and in the cloud by day, to show you the route you should take.' (Dt 1:29-33)

---

4) Just as there is a record of the tree's growth, written in its rings, so there is *a story*, a record, of how our dream unfolds, engraved in us. This story springs from the reality that each person's dream is realised in a unique and constant way.

Our story is often compared in mythology to a thread running through each person's life. This thread has its origin in God and, despite many twists and turns, makes its way back to God, like the river inevitably makes its way to the sea.

> Thee, God, I come from, to thee go,
> All day long I like fountain flow
> From thy hand out, swayed about
> Mote-like in thy mighty glow. (G M Hopkins)

Our story is a record of the very distinctive and constant way God has 'carried' us from our birth, right throughout our lives.

> Listen to me, house of Jacob, all the remnant of the house of Israel, who have been borne by me from your birth, carried from the womb. Even in your old age I will still be the same, and to grey hairs I will carry you. I have made and I will bear; I will carry and will save. (Is 46:3-4)

5) There is *an essential energy* in all things that urges them on towards maturity. The oak tree in Winter may appear to be dead, but come Spring and there is a powerful burst of new life. The Greeks called this energy *eros*, which is one of their words for love. This essentail energy in all things is something that may strike us in the untiring energy with which birds build their nests in Spring, or in the immense vitality we notice in people who fall in love. This energy is a passionate longing in us, a thirst or a hunger that will not be satisfied with anything less than God.

> God, you are my God, I pine for you; my heart thirsts for you, my body longs for you, as a dry weary land without water. (Ps 63:1)

6) This energy constantly draws us on towards *maturity* or wholeness. Just as the dream in the acorn never rests until it is realised in the fully grown oak tree, so the dream in us is restless till it rests in God.

Our dream is that we would realise a vast potential in us for the fullness of life and happiness that God alone can satisfy. His plan is that we would be 'filled with all the fullness of God.' (Eph 3:19) This fullness is described in Jeremiah as a plan God has for our peace.

> For I know the plans I have for you, says the Lord, plans for your peace and not for disaster, to give you a future full of hope. Then you will call upon me and come and pray to me, and I will hear you. You will seek me and find me; when you seek me with all your heart. I will be found by you, says the Lord. (Jr 29:11-14)

7) Our innate dream is not something that will come to be, unless we 'seek it with all our hearts'. It is very different, in this crucial way, from the dream in the oak tree. If ours is to be realized, we have *to get in touch with it* and *take responsibility for bringing it to be.* Many of the parables which Jesus told centre on the importance of our decision to listen to the word of God and put it into practice. Our closeness to Jesus will be proportionate to our willingness to be sensitive and responsive to his word in this way.

> Then his mother and his brothers came to him, but they could not reach him because of the crowd. And he was told, 'Your mother and your brothers are standing outside, wanting to see you.' But he said to them, 'My mother and my brothers are those who hear the word of God and do it.' (Lk 8:19-21)

If we fail to listen to God's word and to take responsibility for it, we will be building our lives on sand.

> But the person who hears me and does nothing about it is like a man who built his house with its foundation upon soft earth. When the flood-water swept down upon it, it collapsed and the whole house crashed down in ruins. (Lk 6:49)

8) It is this capacity, to get in touch with the dream in our heart, and to give it expression in the way we lead our lives, that makes each of us an artist in the deepest sense. The quality of what we produce will depend on our ability to listen to our dream and then to give this expression *in the main work of art each of us is commissioned with.* Realising our dream in this way is the most important and most creative thing we can do in life.

> We are God's work of art, created in Christ Jesus to live the good life as from the beginning he has meant us to live it. (Eph 2:10)

Love as the core of our dream

Very central to the creation story in the book of Genesis is the fact that God has made us in his image. Our dream is the realisation of the immense potential of this image of God in us, of the reality that we are made in the likeness of God.

> Then God said, 'Let us make man in our image, after our likeness; ... So God created man in his own image, in the image of God he created him; male and female he created them. (Gn 1:26-27)

Being made in the likeness of God means that we are similar to one who *is* love. This means that we have an immense capacity to be loved and to return this love. At the core of our dream is an experience, though mainly a dormant one, of 'the love of God flooding through our hearts through the Holy Spirit given to us.' (Rom 5:5)

By pondering the following Greek story, we may get a sense of how basic love is to our dream. It is what makes and sustains us.

Care makes and sustains us

Care was crossing a river one day when she took some soft mud and shaped it into a human being. She wanted to give what she had made her own name but Earth also laid claim to this right. It was, after all, of Earth that the human being was formed. Care then asked Jupiter, who was passing by, to give her creation a spirit. This he gladly agreed to do but then he too wanted it called after him. They decided to ask Saturn to be arbiter and he gave the following decision which seemed a wise one. Jupiter had given it spirit, so he would receive that back when death came. Since it was of earth or humus that it was fashioned, it would be called a human being. However, since Care had formed this human being, it would be her role, as long as this being lived, to sustain it.

This love, symbolised by Care, is not something that we have to earn. It is given as a gift, what Jesus calls the 'gift of God' in Jn 4:10. It is a gift in the sense that it has only to be owned and not earned.

> Just as the Father has loved me, so I have loved you. Remain in my love. (Jn 15:9)

Two symbols of this love

There are two symbols which may help us to understand the love which God has placed at the heart of our dream. They are the symbols of romantic love and friendship. They are symbols which keep cropping up in the Bible when God seeks to tell us what his love is like. The reason for highlighting the two here is that they may help to make the love at the core of our dream more concrete and engaging.

Romantic Love
Romantic love, or the experience of being in love, is one way of expressing what the core of our dream is like. We find this symbol used in the Bible, and by the great Christian writers, to express what is essential to the Christian life. In the Bible, the book which is most associated with romantic love is the Song of Songs. In the monasteries of Europe, it had more commentaries written about it than any other book in the Bible. The people who wrote these commentaries obviously interpreted the dream which inspired their lives in terms of their being in love.

I recently came across an example of how people today interpret their dream in terms of this symbol of romantic love. I was reading Patrick Leigh Fermor' book, *A Time to Keep Silence*. It describes his experiences of visiting five very famous European monasteries. In one of these, curious to find out what drew the monks to their unusual way of life, he says:

> I asked one of the monks how he could sum up, in a couple of words, his way of life. He paused a moment and said, 'Have you ever been in love?' I said, 'Yes'. A large Fernandel smile spread across his face, 'Good', he said, 'It is an exact parallel'.

Judging from how central romantic love is to so many of our stories and films, it would seem to be as central to our secular imagination today as it has been to our religious one. Robert Johnson, in his book *The Psychology of Romantic Love*, holds that romantic love is the greatest source of energy in the western psyche. He sees it as having taken over from religion as our main source of meaning and of ecstasy.

The love of friendship
However, as C S Lewis remarks in his book, *Four Loves*, the falling in love experience has the very serious shortcoming of being the most impermanent of loves. It is, therefore, badly in need of the depth and constancy of the love of *friendship*. This is the second symbol of what is at the core of our dream.

When St Thomas Aquinas wants to describe what it means to be a Christian, he uses the image of friendship. His choice is well founded. It is based on the words of Jesus, 'I have called you friends, because I have told you everything I have heard from the Father.' (Jn 15 15).

Our dream must take on flesh and blood
The purpose of thinking of our dream in terms of romantic love and of friendship is that it might become more tangible and engaging. Our dream, like the Word, must become flesh. If we do not draw on experiences of flesh and blood relationships, our dream can become too abstract. It can remain just an idea in our heads rather than be what fires our hearts. Drawing on our experience of friends, for example, will give us an intimate knowledge of the love which forms the core of our dream.

The Great Commandment that lies at the heart of our dream is that we must strive to take in love and to give it out, with our whole heart and soul, mind and strength. What this commandment requires is that we realise that God is in love with us and that we are invited to respond to this love in a way that is as passionate as any human falling in love. The last few lines of John Donne's poem, *Batter My Heart*, are a marvellous expression of this aspiration.

> Take me to you, imprison mee, for I
> Except you enthral mee, never shall be free,
> Nor ever chaste, except you ravish mee.

Romantic love has the power to get us wholly involved. It brings into play huge resources of energy to be passionate in our quest to bring our dream to be. Friendship, on the other hand, provides a very practical way of going about using this passion or energy to realise our dream. There are few challenges as practical as that of developing the ability to communicate, which is essential to friendship.

Romantic love and friendship, then, help incarnate the love that forms the core of our dream. They lead us, in their distinct ways, to restore an intimacy with God, ourselves and others which we have lost. This intimacy has been restricted or lost because of the way our deep dream has tended to get smothered, due to the dominance of more superficial dreams.

Deep and superficial dreams

Beside the world of our deep dream, or *essence*, there is that of our superficial dream, or *ego*. Unfortunately, the ego world tends to become very domineering because of the excessive demands of the outer world. What happens, for example, when we focus most of our time and energy in pursuit of success? The realisation of our deep dream has to make do with the time and energy that is left over. Thus, in our search for our superficial dream, our deep dream gets drowned out or smothered.

> And the seed sown among the thorns represents the people who hear the word and go on their way, and with the worries, riches and pleasures of living, the life is choked out of them, and in the end they produce nothing. (Lk 8:14)

The Dream Merchant

Nick is employed by a big multinational company as a dream merchant. This means that he spends his time buying and selling dreams. The idea is to get people to trade in their old deep dreams for new superficial ones. The reason why his company employs Nick to do this work is that they realise that when people focus on their deep dream they have little or no desire for what this multinational wants to sell them. If, on the other hand, people can be persuaded to focus on their superficial one, they will be ready to spend their lives working to get the money they will need to buy what Nick's company wants to sell them. They will be open to an endless stream of desire which can be stimulated by the company at will.

Sometimes Nick is a little uneasy about all of this, for he notices that when he buys someone's deep dream, the life seems to go out of them. But overall he thinks his job is justified, for when people concentrate on their deep dream they get too taken up in what is worthwhile in life. In that state they are bad for business.

What removes any misgivings Nick has about his work is that most people are only too willing to do business with him. They obviously find their deep dream a bit unreal and irrelevant to this day and age and it only makes them feel bad having it lying around unused.

Selling your soul

It may be the case that we do not exactly sell our deep dream, but fail to maintain it. The way we get wrapped up in the demands of our outer world may not leave much time for anything else. Then again, there is the fact that the superficial dream of our outer world seems to dictate what is real, significant and worthwhile. Our deep dream thus becomes unreal and irrelevant by comparison. Moreover, it is felt to be abnormal to give much time to our inner selves.

Sin is such a getting out of touch with our deep dream. By becoming separated from our relationships with ourselves, with God and with others, we realise only a small fraction of the potential of the image of God in us.

Arousing our dormant dream

All this resistance to letting our deep dream surface means that it becomes dormant. Our preoccupation with our superficial dream sends our deep one to sleep. However, in spite of this repression our deep dream keeps trying to surface. This constant surging up of our deepest aspirations is due to the fact that we are made for the love which is the object of our deep dream. Further, we are made for a degree of this love which only God can satisfy. This is what St Augustine meant by what must be his most frequently quoted words, 'You have made us for yourself, O Lord, and our hearts will be restless till they rest in you.'

This quest for the realisation of our dream is a hunger that we *are*. We are essentially a hunger for the love which is central to our dream and for the life and happiness which the acceptance of this love brings. It is precisely this hunger which God wishes to satisfy when he reveals himself to us, when he plans to initiate the New Covenant and to make himself known to 'the least no less than to the greatest.' (Jer 31:34) This revelation of himself and our belief in it, is what Jesus describes as the 'work of God'. This work of God centres on the dream which every second of every day of our life God seeks in wonderous ways to realise.

The work of God's providence is his self revelation. By it God seeks to initiate, to establish and to maintain, an intimate relationship of friendship with us. If we co-operate in this work of Providence, we will be led not only to befriend ourselves but others as well as every area of creation. So, when God reveals himself to us he initiates four basic relationships, with himself, ourselves, others and creation. Within these relationships, we can realise our deep dream of being loved and of being loving. Thus God is constantly inviting us on four journeys.

The first journey, on which all the others depend, is that in search of our inmost self. The second journey is inseparable from this for deep within ourselves we will discover that we *are* a thirst for God. It is this thirst which the Trinity seek to satisfy by revealing themselves to us. On the third journey we will seek to befriend others in the way in which the Trinity have befriended us. The fourth journey will be to befriend all those areas of our lives from which we have become estranged and thus to 'bring the good news to the whole of creation.'

On these four journeys towards the realisation of our dream we are constantly accompanied by God. We are accompanied by the the one who constantly inspires our dream; we are accompanied by the one who makes us a hunger for him and plans to satisfy this hunger by the revelation of himself as love; we are accompanied by the one who ceaselessly seeks to lead us into the fullness of his love by enlightening and attracting us. It is hard to find words to convey how profoundly God's providence pervades all our experience, past present and to come. The following are two God-inspired ways of expressing this reality:

I said to you, 'Have no dread or fear of them. The Lord your God, who goes before you, is the one who will fight for you, just as he did for you in Egypt before your very eyes, and in the wilderness, where you saw how the Lord your God carried you, just as one carries a child, all the way that you travelled until you reached this place. But in spite of this, you have no trust in the Lord your God, who goes before you on the way to seek out a place for you to camp, in fire by night, and in the cloud by day, to show you the route you should take.' (Deut 1:29-33)

Listen to me, O house of Jacob, all the remnant of the house of Israel, who have been borne by me from your birth, carried from the womb; even to your old age I am he, even when you turn grey I will carry you. I have made, and I will bear; I will carry and will save. To whom will you liken me and make me equal, and compare me, as though we were alike? (Is 46:3-4)

CHAPTER 2

Setting about realising your dream

In Chapter 1 we saw how our dream differs from the dream in the acorn. We saw that the dream in the acorn is automatically realised, whereas ours only comes to be as a result of our decision. If our dream is to be, we have to get in touch with and then take responsibility for realising it. We have also seen that at the core of our dream is love, which is the essential gift God gives us. (Rom 5:5) So, in order to realise our dream we have to become sensitive and responsive to the way that God in his providence is leading us into the full extent and depth of this love. The method we will use to become more sensitive and responsive to our experience of God's guidance is called reflection.

Reflection

The meaning we give to reflection here is quite different from the analysis of ideas we might normally associate with this word. Throughout this book it will be taken to mean a facility for being in touch with a much wider field of experience than that which our mind alone makes available to us. We might compare this understanding of reflection to awakening areas of our life which have been dormant. From this point of view the meaning of reflection might be clarified by the following story.

Awakenings

The film, from which this true story is taken, is set in a psychiatric hospital in New York. The hospital is for patients who have a disease which leaves them in a sleep-like state. A doctor, whose whole life seems to be lived in his head, comes to the hospital. Through his research, he finds a way of awakening his patients and for a short time they live active and full lives. He cannot, however, keep them like this, so they go back to their sleep-like state again.

At the end of the film the doctor realises that his spirit has undergone an awakening. He sees, through his experience of his care for his patients and the effects of this care on them, that a whole field of experience has been awakened in him. He sees that he must find a way to nourish his spirit and to keep awake whole areas of his life which have been dormant. The film ends with the doctor going out for a cup of coffee with a nurse who had tried, several times during the film, to awaken his heart.

Expanding our horizons

Reflection then is a way of awakening dormant experience. By it we expand our awareness or consciousness of how God's providence is at work, always seeking to realise our dream. Through reflection we become sensitive to the ways God is enlightening our mind and heightening our awareness of the vast amount of experience we have of being loved. We also become aware of the way we are being attracted to respond to God's love. Reflection then is a means of becoming increasingly sensitive and responsive to the way God is enlightening and attracting us.

Reflection assumes that God is a good teacher and has been helping each of us, down through the years, to realise much of our dream. Each of us has, as a result, a huge store of rich and varied experience of being loved and of being loving. Due, however, to the dominance of our superficial dream, our experience of our deep dream is largely dormant. The work of reflection is to arouse it. This is no easy task for we have to contend with a lot of resistance to letting our deep dream surface. This resistance makes reflection a real challenge.

Three stages of reflection

There are three stages of reflection by which we attune ourselves to the way God guides us to fulfil the dream he has for us.

1) We need to *notice* and become increasingly aware of the huge store of experience we have of being loved and of being loving. We thus try to awaken a sense of how effectively God's providence has been at work in us to realise our dream. We also need to notice the signs of God, working in the stream of enlightenment and attraction that runs through each day.

2) Through reflection we also seek to *understand* the way in which God discloses himself to us by gradually enlightening us. We are

thus led to see a vision of God as utterly loving and of ourselves as utterly lovable in his eyes. The effectiveness of this revelation will depend on our willingness to be receptive to and to believe in this true image of God and of ourselves. This willingness will take the form of listening, appreciating and making our own of what God reveals to us.

3) Finally, through reflection we seek to *respond* to the attractions and desires God inspires in us. We will be drawn to respond in words by expressing our gratitude for the gift God gives of himself in self-disclosure. We will be drawn to respond in deeds by letting our minds and hearts be moulded by God's ongoing revelation. This will involve remaining tuned to the way God attracts us to what we are ripe for and to the ways we resist this. We will be constantly led to realise ever more fully the potential of the dream God inspires in us.

Learning from our Experience

In the past, most people were not conscious of the importance of their experience. There has been, however, a revolution in our attitude towards this source of inner wisdom. In my twelve years as a teacher, I witnessed this dramatic change taking place. From having little or no value in the old way of teaching, everyday experience became central in the new one. We moved from the old teacher-centred method, to one centred on the pupils and their personal experience.

For example, in religious education we learned the importance of exploring young people's experience. We found that unless we did this, what we had to teach remained unreal and irrelevant for them. So, within a period of ten years, we moved from the old system of teaching religion, called Religious Knowledge, where experience counted for little, to a new system of religious education, where experience was regarded as central. It was a very difficult change, but one so enlivening that it has influenced everything I have tried to teach since.

In my present work as a spiritual director, helping people to find meaning and direction in their lives, a similar change has taken place. When I was a student, the kind of direction I was given had everything to do with being told the will of God, and very little with what I thought or felt. Now, people's personal experience, the way they feel and what they desire, is where the foundation of all worthwhile spiritual direction is laid.

There is a big change, one might say a revolution, asked of people in this book, for it will be based largely on personal experience. We will be seeking to discover and explore this rich vein of inner wisdom which our personal experience can provide.

Different levels of experience

There are a number of levels of our experience which we will try to get in touch with. What we will be doing will be like digging a well, in order to draw nourishment from our rich, underground stream of inner wisdom.

We will start at the level of our memory of *events,* and then move down to the intuitive, rather than the analytic, *meaning* of these events. These significant events will trigger off *images* in our imaginations. There will be a lot of *feeling* stirred up by the memory of these significant events, and especially by the images we associate with them. Then there will be the level of our *desires* which will indicate the direction in which we are being attracted to move. Finally, through *symbols,* we will try to arouse the deepest level of our experience. Through these symbols we will be helped to get in touch with the riches of the nine tenths of our life which reside in our subconscious and unconscious world.

When we are getting in touch with events, their meaning and the images they arouse, we are working in the area of our mind. When we move to feelings, desires and symbols, we are in the area of our heart.

Getting involved in our experience

An important advantage of getting in touch with these six levels of our experience is that we become much more involved in what is going on in us. This kind of involvement in every level of our experience is what is called for by the Great Commandment. In it we are invited to be loved and to love, not just in a cerebral or unfeeling way, but with 'our whole heart and soul, mind and strength'.

One of the great tragedies of our lives is that we realise so little of this rich potential of the various levels of our experience. As a result, we leave huge areas of our dream unrealised. John Powell has expressed this tragedy in his book, *The Art Of Staying In Love* :

The essential sadness of our human family is that very few of us ever reach the realisation of our full potential. I accept the estimate of the theoreticians that the average person accomplishes only 10% of his potential. ... He is only 10% open to his emotions, to tenderness, to wonder and awe. His mind embraces only a small part of the thoughts, reflections and understanding of which he is capable. His heart is only 10% alive with love. He will die without having really lived or really loved. To me this is the most frightening of all possibilities.

Exercises for reflection on experience
Doing exercises is a way of learning that we are all familiar with from our school days. As adults we may think we have outgrown this procedure. However, I believe there is no better way of going about changing our minds and hearts than by taking a small amount of what we want to learn and doing exercises with it. In this way we gain a much deeper understanding than by merely thinking about it.

Where I experienced most profoundly the effectiveness of this way of proceeding was in a book of spiritual exercises by Ignatius Loyola. As a way of expressing his profound spiritual experience, Ignatius chose not to write a book that would have been a theoretical explanation of what happened to him as a spiritual pilgrim. Rather he wrote a book of spiritual exercises. In it he says to us, in effect, 'Do these exercises and I feel sure that you will have a similar experience to mine.' Through the exercises, he hoped that we would see, from reflecting on our own unique experience of doing them, something of the profound vision he was led to see.

Two traditions
This approach, of learning from the experience of doing exercises, is a return to a tradition that deeply influenced people for nine centuries preceding St Ignatius' time. These people trusted personal experience born of prayer and reflection, more than the kind of knowledge gained from the study of ideas in theological writings.

In a book called, *The Love of Learning and the Desire for God*, Jean Leclercq gives us the fruit of his study of two traditions that we are heir to. The earlier of these was a monastic tradition and its aim was wisdom, or an intimate knowledge of God. This wisdom was sought mainly through the experience of four steps of a prayer exercise which was later called the ladder of the monk. The later tradition of the Scholastics, which has predominated since the middle ages, aims at what is a more exterior knowledge. This is achieved through rational analysis or speculation.

These two traditions, and especially the earlier monastic one with its emphasis on prayer, are neglected today. This is clearly stated in the following quotation from *A Survey of Religious Attitudes and Beliefs* by Máire Nic Ghiolla Phádraig (1975).

> Where the Irish Catholic Church is weakest is in the basic area of 'religious experience' and prayer – the mystical dimension. This is probably because it has never been considered a pastoral priority, seeing that the 'faith of the simple people' was so strong. The main emphasis was towards strengthening the institutional church; marginal effort was put into strengthening the intellectual basis of the Church's pastoral presence, and the prayer, religious experience, mystical element was given the lowest priority rating. The figure for the prayer patterns among the young today indicate that this is a task which can no longer be postponed. The Church will be in a strong position only when all three elements are given due weight.

The stress in this book, therefore, will be on what we can learn by reflecting on our personal experience of doing exercises. I hope that this approach will help you to discover, explore and take possession of your deep dream, so that it may influence every area of your life.

The Exercises

The exercises are divided into five parts.

1) In Exercises 1-4 of Part I, the focus will be on our story. We will reflect on its development during the various stages of our lives. Alongside this consciousness of our own story, we will cultivate a sense of the reality of God being with us all along the way we travel. As we have seen, our story is part of a plan that God is constantly helping us realise. We will discern this plan in the recurring patterns of God's enlightenment and attraction. In these patterns we may hope to find the vision and the values which give our life meaning and direction. We will conclude Part I by building a bridge to Part II. We will look at the reality that 90% of our story is good, but that it is easy to let the 10% that is not so good dominate our attention.

2) In Exercises 5-10 of Part II, we will look at the way our dream has to be realised in the imperfect world of our human limitations and waywardness. We will see how the experience of our poverty can be constructive or destructive, in that it can build up our faith or erode it. The experience of our poverty can help the realisation of our dream or hinder it.

We will also cultivate a growing consciousness of how we are influenced, in healthy and unhealthy ways, by our daily experience of our poverty. We will finish Part II by focusing on two forms of therapy, one long-term, and the other short-term. Through these two therapies we will see how we can heal the wounds inflicted by the destructive interpretation of our poverty.

3) In Exercises 11-17 of Part III, we will focus on the love that is the core of our dream. We will start by focusing on our experience of four loves that are central to our dream. We will then concentrate on each of these loves in turn, starting with the love of the significant people who have believed in us. The main stress, however, will be on our experience of being loved by each of the persons of the Trinity. We will see how the Father seeks to disclose himself to each person as love, how Jesus expresses this love in human terms, and how the Spirit leads us into an interior knowledge of the extent and depth of God's love for all creation. We will then conclude Part III by reflecting on how we have responded to this love.

4) In Exercises 18-28 of Part IV, we will see how we are to bring the Good News of God's love to all creation. This extension of the Good News to every area of life is to counteract the mentality which confines us to a tiny world. Therefore, we will seek to befriend all those areas of God's creation from which we have become estranged.

5) Finally, in Exercises 29-30 of Part V, we will examine how, by tuning in to our desires and by making decisions we can take responsibility for bringing our dream to be. Where up to this the focus will have been on discovering, exploring and making our own of our dream, we will in these two final exercises focus on how we must take responsibility for integrating our dream into the way we live.

CHAPTER 3

Capturing Your Dream

In Chapter 1 we saw that if our dream is to be realised we have to get in touch with it and take responsibility for it. Then in Chapter 2 we examined a way of setting about realising our dream through reflection on our experience. In this chapter, we will focus on *journaling* as a specialised way of reflecting on our experience. As journaling will be the method used in every exercise in this book, we need to spend time becoming familiar with it. So we will examine the kind of experience journaling deals with, and the way it goes about reflecting on this experience. Finally, we will look at some guidelines for the way we approach journaling.

The person with whom journaling is most closely associated today is Ira Progoff. He became aware of the limitations of focusing on the analysis of what went wrong in people's past. What he saw as an alternative to this arose from work he did on the lives of creative people. Through his study of these people, he realised the central importance of working with the creative potential which is built into each of us. To help people realise this potential, he devised what he called the intensive journal. This is a way of getting people to process, in a creative way, the immense potential that lies dormant in their own experience.

The following story is one which I think Progoff would like. It focuses on the possibilities of dealing with life's problems through working with feelings and fantasy rather than through the rational analysis of our problems.

Southwell's medicine
Robert Southwell was a Jesuit priest who lived in England during the reign of Queen Elizabeth I. During her reign, the Catholic Church was persecuted and Southwell as one of its priests was hunted and would have been executed if he had been caught. Priests like him survived because they found refuge in

the homes of Catholic families. However, if these families were discovered harbouring a priest, they would lose all they possessed.

There was one family who gave shelter to Southwell until the lady of the house became so fearful of the consequences of being caught that she told Southwell that he could no longer hide in her home. He said he respected the position she found herself in but he asked her to postpone her decision for six months. He told her that he would go elsewhere for the six months and that he would willingly respect her decision at the end of that time. He recommended that she should prepare for her decision by doing an exercise.

The exercise consisted in imagining that she was discovered hiding a priest. She was to dwell at length on all the consequences, the sequence of events and the images and the feelings these would give rise to. She was then to weigh up the pros and cons of allowing him to continue to find refuge from his persecutors in her house.

When Southwell returned at the end of the agreed time, she told him that he was most welcome to continue to use her house as a refuge at any time he wanted to do so.

Four kinds of experience

✓ Journaling is a means of getting in touch with the full range of our experience. It focuses on the events of our story and the meaning we may discover in these events. It also focuses on the feelings and the images which the events of our story arouse. There are <u>four</u> areas of our experience of our dream which our journal will help us to explore. These are the *sensory*, the *reflective*, the *feeling* and the *intuitive* areas. Their ultimate importance is that they are <u>four</u> key ways in which we are invited <u>to take in love</u> and to <u>give it out</u> and thus to fulfil our dream.

1) *The factual or sensory area of our experience* is where we become familiar with the <u>concrete</u> events of our life. The journal seeks to link these events together to discover our story as the record of the way our dream has unfolded. As we saw in Chapter 1, this unfolding of our dream takes place in a unique and consistent way throughout our life.

As we recall the events of our story, list, describe, and even re-live them, we get inside our story and perceive it from within. We thus cease to be an observer looking in from the outside, as we are when we think about the details of our past in an analytic way. It is by walking around inside our story, in the way that journaling allows us to do, that we get a very tangible sense of our identity.

2) As we remember and write about the events of our life, they reveal their significance to us. We thus move to the *reflective area of our experience*. As we move back through the events of our story we will notice a growing capacity to find new meaning and direction emerging from these events. We gain a facility in understanding our life more and more in the context of our story. We will also gain a facility in discerning where we are going, through our aspirations, desires and hopes for the future. It is by looking back on the path our life has followed that we gather the insight into where we should be moving and the momentum to do so. This growing sense of the meaning and direction of our life is more the fruit of intuition and of listening than of analytical thought.

Since our dream unfolds in a unique and constant way, there is a consistency in our outlook on life in the different periods of our story. The journal will help us discover this persistent vision we have developed in the course of our story, as well as the ways we have modified this vision from one period of our story to another.

3) When we describe or re-live the events of our story with the help of our journal, we will notice that these events stir up a lot of feeling in us. This *feeling area of our experience* is encountered at two levels, especially when we are challenged by life. At such times we may feel emotionally upset at an upper level, but at a deeper level, where our convictions about what is worthwhile reside, we may feel at peace. These convictions form the values which are unique to each person's story. Our values like our vision, are constant and yet we modify them somewhat from one period of our story to another.

Journaling this feeling area of our experience is more difficult than journaling our sensory and reflective areas of experience. This may be because our feelings have been repressed as a result of the belief that they do not count. We may also have been led to believe that the way we feel is secondary to, and must therefore not interfere with, the logic or objectivity of our thought.

The good feelings we will be cultivating through journaling will be ones like wonder, appreciation, joy and gratitude. It is hoped that by becoming aware of our positive feelings and sharing them, that we may intensify and thus give them a more dominant role in our life. Our negative feelings, such as anger, guilt, fear and anxiety, are inclined to hold our attention and dominate the way we see things. So we will be seeking a better balance by becoming aware of our negative feelings and by thus getting freedom from their dominance. This will allow us to make more room for our positive feelings. When we develop our awareness of this feeling, or heart level of experience, we will be in a good position to enter into the dialogues which are the high point of most of the exercises in this book.

4) *The intuitive level of our experience* is the deepest one. It is here that the distilled wisdom of the conscious areas of our experience is stored in the form of symbols. These symbols are our main source of contact with our underground stream of inner wisdom. It is through writing about these symbols, and the images and fantasies associated with them, that we get in touch with our unconscious world. This world is a very large and rich one, for it is here that we store the nine tenths of our experience, which like the iceberg, lie well below the surface.

When we get in touch with images and symbols, we do what dreams do, that is we draw on the unconscious for what we need to give our life meaning and direction. The line of a song, or a story we come across in a novel, or in a film, may find an echo in our depths where a part of us calls out to be attended to. It is in this intuitive area of our experience that our dream can be grasped much more satisfyingly than it can be rationally understood.

Journaling as a method of reflection

We now turn to look at ways in which we can make our own of our rich store of experience by journaling it. The way we will go about this can be compared to going on an inner journey on which we discover and take possession of the jewel we have in our dream.

The journey in search of the jewel

There was once a man who came across a cave on his journey and, being curious, he entered it. Within the cave he discovered what was to be the inspiration of his life, in the form of a priceless jewel. However, all he could do was gaze at the jewel for it was held firmly in the grasp of a ferocious beast. As he gazed at the precious stone, his whole being was engaged. When eventually he decided that he must leave the cave and continue on his journey, he felt that all else in life from then on would be insignificant by comparison with what he had discovered in the cave.

During the years that followed, even though he was preoccupied with his work and with rearing his family, he never forgot the vision he had seen in the cave as a young man. This always remained an inspiration and became more and more an essential part of his life. When eventually his work was done and his family reared, he said to his wife, 'Before I die, I must glimpse again the jewel that has been the inspiration of my life.'

So he set out and made his way back to the cave where he again found the jewel. But now the monster guarding it had grown so small that he was able to take the jewel away with him. As he made his way back home, he gradually realised the meaning of what had happened. He realised that the jewel was but a symbol of something he had discovered in himself. It was to take possession of this jewel that he had been struggling all his life with the ferocious beast.

This journey in search of our jewel is one on which we seek to discover, explore and take possession of the 'the gift of God'. (Jn 4:10) This gift is the love of God, or what we call Grace, and it is the object of our dream. Our journey in search of the jewel can be understood in terms of a growing consciousness of the extent and depth of the love of God and of how we might best respond to this love. There are a number of levels of this consciousness which we will be seeking to explore by means of our journal. The following is an outline of four of these levels of consciousness.

Heightening our awareness
If we are to express our experience on paper, as is essential to journaling, we have not only to become aware of the details of our experience but to put words on it. We have not only to be attentive to our experience but to name it. When we thus *heighten our awareness* of the events of our story, positive and negative feelings are bound to arise. We need to notice, name and share these. By responding to our feelings in this way, we will intensify the positive

ones and we will gain a greater degree of freedom from being dominated by the negative ones.

At this initial level of consciousness, by noticing, naming and sharing our experience, we initiate a relationship with the area of experience which we are journaling. Journaling thus helps us to discover a fund of wisdom which we have learned from these relationships which constitute our inner world. This is a very valuable resource but one which we can easily leave dormant. If we do, we will fail to acknowledge the inner eventfulness of what might seem to be an uneventful life.

Attaining an intimate understanding
There is a very distinct way in which journaling helps us to *understand* the events of our story. The effort to articulate our experience of these events has a unique capacity to clarify what might otherwise remain vague. When we struggle to write about our experience, we gain a more intimate understanding of it than if we just think about it. When we journal our experience, there is a sense of walking around within it. We get to know what our experience feels like from the inside. Progoff sees journaling as an inward movement by which we get inside the events of our story. By listing, describing and re-living these events, we gain what might be called a *felt* knowledge of them. Journaling thus leads to an interior or intimate knowledge, whereas analysing the events of our story in a thinking way leads to the more abstract, exterior knowledge of the detached observer.

When we journal, we are not only seeking to gain an interior knowledge of our life but to know ourselves in depth. There is a downward movement as well as an inward one. So throughout the exercises, we will be drawing on the riches of our unconscious with the help of imagery, fantasies and through dialogues with the wisdom figures in our life. By reaching down into our depths in this way, we gain an extraordinary insight into the unique movement of our life, into where we have come from and into where we are called to move.

Appropriating our experience
Journaling helps us to *assimilate* those parts of our experience which we are ready to make our own of. How the journal helps us to digest the experience we are ripe for is similar to the way we can digest the significant things that our dreams of the night want

to say to us. So, for example, when we wake up in the morning we are sometimes aware of having had a very vivid dream. It is striking how quickly the details of the dream fade unless we write them down soon after we have had the dream. If we do record our dream, even the barest outline of it, we then have the valuable insight expressed in our dream permanently available to us. We can go back to our dream at any time to appropriate it more fully.

We can realise our deep dream only bit by bit. What bit of our dream we are ready to make our own of, will be indicated by the kind of enlightenment and desire which is prominent at any stage of our life. We will be constantly challenged to make our own of some aspect of the love which is central to our dream. We will be challenged to make our own of this love by listening and responding to it and so letting it mould our mind and heart. We will try, in the exercises, to assimilate what is central for us in our experience, with the help of mantras and symbols and especially with the help of the dialogues and prayer which will be the high point of each exercise. Progroff devotes a large part of his work on journalling to Process Meditation. This is a way of absorbing what is particularly significant in our experience.

Transforming our life
Journaling provides a very concrete way of taking responsibility for realising our dream. It creates a space in our life where we can listen to our experience and give a healthy expression to the feelings which this experience arouses. This kind of listening and responding is the most effective way of changing our minds and hearts. By listening, we expose and adjust our minds to the truth so that we gradually absorb it and let it mould our outlook. By responding honestly, our hearts are freed from what blocks our acceptance of the truth.

By developing our capacity to listen and to respond, journaling helps us to open up to the relationships which are central to our dream. God initiates these relationships by revealing himself to us. It is then up to us to co-operate in establishing and maintaining these relationships by listening and responding to God's self disclosure. As we move down through the seven or so parts of each exercise we will be building up our ability to communicate. The ultimate objective of this communication will be to relate intimately with that area of our life which we are seeking to befriend in the particular exercise. Progoff is convinced that when we, as individuals, dig our well, and so reach our underground stream, we discover a place which is conducive to intimacy with others. ✓

A way of writing the journal

From what we have seen so far, journaling may seem very formidable. However, it is not as demanding as it may seem. The following guidelines, for the kind of writing involved in journaling, may help to release us from the fear which can block our efforts to journal.

a) The internal censor

There should be no judgment passed on what we write. It is essential to say what we want to, without imposing any censorship on what we say. We are brought up to exercise a reserve with regard to what we say to others. The result is that we suppress a lot of what it would be healthier for us to admit, at least to ourselves. For example, we might feel like saying strong feelings but suppress them, for fear of disturbing the peace – our own as well as that of others. In journaling, we remove the censor and say what ✓ we want, secure in the fact that it is for our eyes alone.

The internal censor is very critical of the content of what we write. ℕ𝓑 It is all the time editing what we may or may not say. In this way it becomes one of the blocks which most frequently prevents us from journaling or which soon paralyses us even if we do get started. There are certain tactics which we can use in order to avoid the internal censor. We need to be aware of the wisdom of writing quickly everything which comes into our head. We should not be deterred when the internal censor labels something as being not 'nice' or 'inappropriate' and therefore better left unsaid. It is especially important not to stifle our intuitions and feelings by being guarded about our secret thoughts and emotions.

b) The internal critic

There is an inner voice which is very critical of the quality of what we say. We normally write out of our heads and therefore, accuracy in the way we express ourselves is a high priority. With journaling, spontaneity will be more important than any effort to write our thoughts correctly. So we will need to be ready to note down what comes to us, in whatever way we find it easiest to express ourselves. For example, we will be dealing a lot with feelings, images and symbols and these are of their nature vague. If we are waiting to express ourselves clearly before we put pen to paper, we will be paralysed by writer's block. So we should say what we want to, in any way that suggests itself to us.

When I was a student I tried to record my reflections of a very eventful holiday I had, touring Scotland on a bicycle. I never got past the first paragraph, as I was so critical of the way I was saying things. I was paralysed by my inability to write stylishly what I was bursting to say. So, we should say what we want to in any old way, creating our own abbreviations and ways of expressing ourselves that will ease the flow of our experience onto paper.

c) Don't give too much of yourself away!
The traditional diary keeps things very factual and on the surface. The journal helps us to move inwards and downwards. Its aim is to help us to discover and to come to know our true self so that we do not need to wear a mask or play a role. If we are to discover this true self, we have to get in touch with how we really feel and think, with what we really believe and desire.

People often think of this kind of probing our depths as something achieved by means of a deep analysis of the hang-ups from our past. Journaling focuses much more on what is positive and on the potential that we find in our depths than on any kind of analysis of the negative. Throughout the exercises, we will focus on our feelings and on our images as where the deeper side of ourselves is revealed. Our feelings want to reveal to us our unique inner world, and the images called up by the events of our life constantly seek to put us in touch with the riches of our unconscious world.

d) Feedback
One of the great benefits of the kind of spontaneous writing journaling encourages, is cross-fertilization. This is the capacity of one thought or image to generate another. Facilitating this through re-reading what we have written is a major feature of journaling. An alternative procedure to re-reading is to record what we have written and then to play it back.

Conclusion
In these three introductory chapters, we started out with the notion of our inbuilt dream and we have finished up with a description of journaling as a practical method of realising it.

We have seen that our dream is to realise all the potential of the image of God in us. This means bringing to full flower all the potential in us to be loved and to love. God seeks to realise our dream by revealing his love for us and by gradually guiding us into its full extent and depth. For our part, we have to listen and respond to this guidance by reflecting on our experience of the Spirit enlightening and attracting us. We choose journaling as a specialised method of reflecting on this experience. With its help we can gradually expand our conscious grasp of God's love and providence and so realise our dream.

We will finish off with Ira Progoff's statement of what for him is the objective of journalling.

> When a person is shown how to reconnect himself with the contents and the continuity of his life, the inner thread of movement by which his life has been unfolding reveals itself to him by itself. Given the opportunity, a life crystallises itself out of its own nature, revealing its meaning and its goal. (*The Intensive Journal*, Ira Progoff.)

PART 1

Introduction to Exercises 1-4

Discovering our inner self
The underlying problem we face today is self alienation. This is
the conclusion which John Powell comes to in his book, *A Reason
to Live, A Reason to Die,* in which he tries to discover what is the essential malaise which is afflicting us today. This self alienation
means that we are strangers to our true self and unable to enter
the inner world of our dream. In this first part of the book we will
be developing a facility to disengage ourselves from excessive
preoccupation with the expectations of our outer world. We will
do this in order to enter our inner world. This may appear to be a
world of fantasy but it is where we find our deep dream.

Going Bear-hunting
There was this sociologist who was making a study of some
North American Indians. One day she was present when a government official was lecturing in a particular village on the
necessity of digging proper latrines. The sociologist noticed
that one of the Indians burst out laughing at a very boring part
of the lecture. She was curious about this, so after the official
had gone, she asked the Indian what was so amusing. He said,
'Oh, the bear had just fallen into the water'. When she enquired
further she found that every time he became bored, especially
with talks from government officials, he would, in his imagination, go bear hunting, to enjoy all the excitement of it.

Escaping to reality
The Indian did not find, in the official's message, much to hold his
attention or to engage his spirit. He needed, therefore, to escape to
an inner world, a world of the spirit. This was much more real and
involving than the outer world in which the government official
was seeking to engage him.

What is symbolised by going bear hunting in this story is our
need to keep in touch with the inner world of our dream. This is

difficult as we live in an atmosphere in which our inner world is dominated by our outer world of work and leisure. The result is that our inner world has been diminished and has become unreal. However, our inner world, no matter how we suppress it, keeps trying to assert itself and to right the destructive imbalance between it and our outer world.

Exploring our story

The best way to enter our inner world is through our story. This is a record of how our dream has unfolded. It is written in our imaginations and in our feelings, in our minds and in our hearts. Since our story has such power to reveal our inner self, and to engage our whole person in coming to know ourselves, we will devote the first four exercises to our story.

Exercise 1 aims at helping us to get to know our inner self better, through becoming more familiar with our story.

Exercise 2 aims at keeping alive the reality that the most significant aspect of our story is that, throughout it, God in his providence guides us towards the realisation of our dream.

Exercise 3 seeks to discover something of the unique outlook or vision which we have been led to by God and which gives meaning to our life.

Exercise 4 focuses on two basic aspects of ourselves which emerge from our story. We will see how vitally important it is for us to live with these two, with the ideal as well as the shadow side of ourselves.

Your own story

If a tree is cut down, we have all the evidence – if we could read it – for writing its story. The narrative of all its days is written into the rings that represent the yearly periods of the tree's history. The stresses and strains of storms, and all the circumstances that have affected the tree's growth, will be recorded in this story of how the tree's dream unfolded.

Like the tree, our story is recorded within us, in our bodies, minds and hearts. Who we are, the enlightenments and desires that are the gradual unfolding of our dream, are all written there. The record of this, stretching back into our past and on into our future, can be compared to an underground stream of inner wisdom running through our lives.

Drawing on our stream of inner wisdom
Nobody can discover for us this store of wisdom that lies in our underground stream. This is because our inner wisdom, like our deep dream, is unique. No two people are led along the same road towards the fulfilment of their dream.

If we want to draw on the rich resources which we have in our underground stream of inner wisdom, we have to dig our own well to reach them. It is as if our underground stream is fed by the different layers of our experience which, like tributaries, feed our stream of wisdom. By digging our well we get in touch with the wisdom that lies in each of these layers of our experience.

A method of digging your well
This exercise is a way of discovering and exploring your stream of unique inner wisdom and the way it manifests how your dream has been unfolding. Before you begin the exercise, it may be necessary to remind yourself again of the guidelines for journaling. Here is an outline of the most important points:

It is important that what you say, as you journal, and the way you

---

say it, is spontaneous and not guarded or censored – normally, we have to calculate carefully what we can safely say and how we say it. With no concern, therefore, for what you say or how you say it, jot down in words or phrases what comes to mind as you work your way through the different parts of the exercise.

Read back regularly through what you have written and notice if this stimulates some fresh material you wish to add, or whether you wish to change what you have already written.

THE EXERCISE

1) Whenever you journal, there should be a period of preparation. This should take the form of a quietening and centring exercise which is meant to give you time to slow down and to become focused.

Begin by fixing your attention on something concrete or tangible. This might be some object before you or it could be your breathing or a part of your body that you focus your attention on. For now, let your gaze rest on some object before you and focus on that. Allow all else to slip into the background. If other concerns emerge, gently shift your attention back onto the object you are trying to make the focus of your attention. You will notice that most of what has been occupying your attention will let go its hold on you and that you will become more relaxed. It is important that you do not force yourself to suddenly let go of everything which has been occupying your mind. This excessive effort may build up its own tension and defeat the purpose of the exercise. Be satisfied to gradually become a little more relaxed and focused.

When you have grown still, shift your attention to some inner reality that is important for you just now. This will normally be supplied by the introduction to each of the exercises you will be doing. But for the exercise you are doing just now, focus your attention on a simple statement of the inner reality you want to stay with. This might be your desire to make time to be apart. So you might put your desire in a short statement like, 'I want to take time apart'. Repeat this slowly, over and over again to yourself. When you have finished, spend a little time noticing how you feel and note this down.

2) Describe an important event in your life. Say why this event is significant for you, and what you learned from what happened.

Does it bring home to you anything about yourself which is new to you or which you have not noticed before?

Re-read your description of the event. Note down any positive feelings and then any negative feelings which recalling the event and describing it arouses in you. For example, recalling the event may cause you to re-live the enthusiasm you felt at the time, but there may also be a sense of disillusionment which you now associate with it. Describe the images you connect with the event. These images are memories you think of in connection with the event and can be things you saw, heard, smelt or were touched by at the time of the event. These intuitions, feelings and images may trigger off deep experiences within you. If you become conscious of any of these, try to describe one and note how doing this makes you feel.

3) List the *significant events* which have been prominent in your recent experience. (Take 'recent' to mean whatever length of time forms the boundary of this present period of your life.) Take the time you need to make as full a list as you can and then underline the more important events.

4) Describe the significance of some of these events. Is there a wisdom you have learned from them? We get *insights* about life that go to make up our store of common sense or wisdom. However, this wisdom may lie dormant and may take a lot of patient effort to arouse.

5) What *images* do you associate with any of these events? Images can come, for example, in the form of a line of a song, the words of a poem, in a favourite verse of Scripture, in a picture or an expressive word. Dreams, films, books, and your daily experience will supply you with images from which to choose.

6) Do the above events, ideas and images arouse any *feelings* in you? Are your feelings mixed, or just positive? Initially, these feelings may be quite difficult to notice and to name but it is worth the effort as they are a very distinctive part of you. Choose one recent happening which moved you and share how you feel about it with yourself or with someone you imagine as present.

7) List some of the *attractions or desires* which you notice surfacing for you as you look at what has been going on in your life recently. Do you notice any aspirations or deep ambitions that are

giving your life direction at present? What are your long and short term priorities just now?

8) The deepest level of your experience is expressed most profoundly by *symbols*. These are images which have a lot of meaning and feeling wrapped up in them. If you were asked to choose a symbol which would capture a lot of the meaning and feeling connected with the events you have recorded, which one would you choose? It could be expressed in a line of a poem, a verse from Scripture or in the form of a line drawing or a diagram. How ould you explain to someone what this symbol means for you and how you feel about it?

This symbolic level of your experience is the most difficult to express but it can also be the richest. So, any time you spend working on the symbols of your life will be well worthwhile.

Feeling God's finger

What role do we see providence playing in our story? The answer that is most ready to hand today is that of a world view and value system generated by science, economics and our consumer culture. In this view there is a loss of consciousness and appreciation of God's plan and its influence on our daily experience. God's providence is peripheral; it has ceased to matter. What does matter is in fact an illusion that we are in control of our life, a life which is bounded by our material living conditions. Yet the human spirit is not content to be confined to this very limited vision of reality. It looks for more meaning and direction in life than the material world bereft of providence can provide.

Imprisoned in a small world
In AD 627 the monk Paulinus visited King Edwin in northern England to persuade him to accept christianity. Before making a decision, the king thought to consult his advisors. After they had discussed the matter at length, one advisor stood up and said, 'Your majesty, when you sit at table with your lords and vassals, in the winter, when the fire burns warm and bright on the hearth and the storm is howling outside, bringing the snow and the rain, it happens of a sudden that a little bird flies into the hall. The bird flies in through one door and flies out through the other. For the few moments that it is inside the hall, the bird does not feel the cold, but as soon as it leaves your sight, it returns to the dark of winter. It seems to me that the life of man is much the same. We do not know what went before and we do not know what follows. If the new doctrine can speak to us of these things, it is well for us to follow it'.

Seeing the big picture
'The new doctrine' is the Good News. Accepting it involves changing our minds and hearts in order to believe in the reality

---

that our lives are pervaded by God's love and providence. Our story becomes part of this much bigger picture of reality when seen in the light of God's plan for our peace. (Jer 29:11) When this plan or God's dream for us becomes a priority it gives ultimate meaning to our story and a sense of direction for the future. This sense of providence pervading our story is strikingly expressed in the following passage from the book of Deuteronomy:

> I said to you, 'Have no dread or fear of them. The Lord your God, who goes before you, is the one who will fight for you, just as he did for you in Egypt before your very eyes, and in the wilderness, where you saw how the Lord your God carried you, just as one carries a child, all the way that you travelled until you reached this place. But in spite of this, you have no trust in the Lord your God, who goes before you on the way to seek out a place for you to camp, in fire by night, and in the cloud by day, to show you the route you should take.' (Deut 1:29-33)

This view of providence is one we are invited to see as permeating the past, the present and the future.

> And now I am about to go the way of all the earth, and you know in your hearts and souls, all of you, that not one thing has failed of all the good things which the Lord your God promised concerning you; all have come to pass for you, not one of them has failed. (Jos 23:14)

> Listen to me, O house of Jacob, all the remnant of the house of Israel, who have been borne by me from your birth, carried from the womb; even to your old age I am He, even when you turn grey I will carry you. I have made, and I will bear; I will carry and will save. (Is 46:3-4)

> We know that in everything God works for good with those who love him, who are called according to his purpose. (Rom 8:28-29)

Most of us begin life with the conviction that we can control our destiny, we feel that we are the captain of our soul. The shape our life takes seems to be 90% our doing and 10% God's. Life's frustrations, however, and a growing realisation of our limitations tends to reverse these proportions. We are led to the conviction that 'There's a divinity that shapes our ends, Rough hew them how we will.' (Shakespeare)

With an anvil-ding
And with fire in him forge thy will
Or rather, rather then, stealing as Spring
Through him, melt him but master him still:
Whether at once, as once at a crash Paul,
Or as Austin, a lingering-out sweet skill,
Make mercy in all of us, out of us all
Mastery, but be adored, but be adored King. (G M Hopkins)

A world pervaded by Providence

When I look back on my parents' world, I am struck by their sense of life being in God's hands at the time. I found their convictions about everything being God's will hard to understand. My life then seemed to me to be of my own making and God's role in it seemed peripheral. Now in the second half of my life I find myself more attuned to their sense of life being pervaded by providence.

This exercise seeks to raise our consciousness and appreciation of God's Providence in our story. The most important dimension of our story is that God is active in every detail of it, helping us to realise the dream he has built into us. In this exercise, therefore, we will focus our attention on a method of becoming more sensitive and responsive to the way God's providence influences us. This method, called reflection, will build up our facility to prayerfully advert to Providence's role in realising our dream. Through this practice of reflection we will try to live with the reality that God 'has been with us all along the way we have travelled on our journey to this place.' (Deut 1:31) If we lose touch with this reality we will miss the real significance of what is happening in our story.

Thou mastering me
God! giver of breath and bread;
World's strand, sway of the sea;
Lord of living and dead;
Thou hast bound bones and veins in me, fastened me flesh,
And after it almost unmade, what with dread,
Thy doing: and dost thou touch me afresh?
Over again I feel thy finger and find thee. (G M Hopkins)

Realising God is with us all along the way

The most important dimension of our story is that God is active in every detail of it, helping us to realise the dream he has planted in us. Throughout this book it will, therefore, be essential to keep prayerfully adverting to the reality that God 'has been with us all along the way we have travelled on our journey to this place.' (Deut 1:31) If we lose touch with this reality, we will lose the real significance of what is happening in our story.

THE EXERCISE

1) What does the fact that God is provident mean to you? Does it mean that God cares for you? What form does God's care for you take? Is this care more like the way your father or the way your mother looked after you? In the present period of your story do you find much of a role for the providence of God in it? Note down the images, feelings, desires and the symbol which you associate with your present understanding of God's providence.

2) Does your present view of the way God looks after you differ much from the way you saw God doing this at other times in your life? Go back to times in your life when this aspect of God was challenged. Notice what images, feelings and expectations you then had with regard to providence. Would the statement that no detail in your life is too insignificant for God to concern himself with sound improbable for you now? How would this statement have sounded to you when you were in your teens?

3) What way do you think of God as influencing your life? Do you feel God is more concerned with the way you behave than with the way you see life and with the way you feel about it?

If we take it that God is calling us to repent and believe the Good News and that repentance means changing our minds and hearts, how does God go about helping us with this kind of change? Describe the way you think God sets about helping you to change your mind and see whether you notice this happening to you. Do you notice yourself being enlightened, that you are moved to see new things or to see old insights anew? Does God enlighten you an odd time or is God always influencing you in this way? Draw a circle and see what percentage of it represents the enlightenment you find and the enlightenment God brings about in you. Do the percentages differ in theory and in practice?

4)What way does God seek to influence your heart? Describe how you notice this influence. Does it seem to take place the whole time, often, or only the odd time? Do you attribute much of the feelings, the attractions and the desires which you notice in your story to God's influence? Ponder the following passage of scripture in the light of what you have written so far in this part of the exercise.

> And he (Jacob) dreamed that there was a ladder set up on the earth, and the top of it reached to heaven; and behold the angels of God were ascending and descending on it. And behold, the Lord stood above it and said, ... 'See, I am with you and will keep you wherever you go, and will bring you back to this land; for I will not leave you until I have done that of which I have spoken to you'. Then Jacob awoke from his sleep and said, 'Surely the Lord is in this place; and I did not know it'. And he was afraid and said, 'How awesome is this place! This is none other than the house of God; this is the gate of heaven'. (Gn 28:12-13,15-17

5) A diagram may help you clarify the way your notion of providence is changing. If you could, imagine people's early notions of providence as represented by a small circle within a larger one. The large circle represents their outer world to which they give most of their time and attention. As people move on through life they often come to see their world of outer activity as the small circle which is within the larger one which now represents God's providence. See which of the two diagrams you identify most with at present and then depict this on paper.

6) In this final part of this exercise we will look at how, through three steps of reflection we might in a practical way heighten our awareness of God's providence in our lives.

Re-read what you wrote in Exercise 1 about any event in your story. Then:

a) Notice and write down what strikes you, anything you see clearly, what attracts you, or what appeals to your mind, to your heart, or to your imagination.

How important it is for us to notice the signs of God at work in us can be appreciated from the following parable. Ponder it for a while.

> And he told them a parable: Look at the fig tree, and all the trees; as soon as they come out in leaf, you see for yourselves and know that the summer is already near. So also, when you

see these things taking place, you know that the kingdom of God is near. (Lk 21: 29-31)

b) Discern or try to understand the reality that God had a hand in the fact that something struck you or in your being attracted in a certain way. So spend time prayerfully identifying God as the one who has enlightened you. In this way, you might move away from seeing all that happens as your own doing, and towards a deeper realization that this is the way God is guiding you.

Spend some time with the following passages seeking to appreciate the importance of this stage of reflection.

Do you not yet perceive or understand? Are your hearts hardened? Having eyes do you not see, and having ears do you not hear. And do you not remember? When I broke the loaves for the five thousand, how many baskets full of broken pieces did you take up? ... Do you not yet understand? (Mk 8:17-21)

I planted, Apollos watered, but God gave the growth. So he who plants nor he who waters is anything, but only God who gives the growth. ... For we are God's fellow workers; you are God's field, God's building. (1 Co 3: 6-9)

c) Respond to this reality of God pointing out something as important for you now, by listening to and making your own of it. It is impossible for God to guide or to teach us anything unless we are willing to spend time taking it in and digesting it. God will want you to walk around in what he opens up for you and so he will not flood you with new insights and desires. If he did, you would never learn anything properly. So, continue patiently to dig where you find gold.

Spend time pondering the importance of this third stage of reflection with the help of the following verse from the parable of the sower:

And as for that in the good soil, they are those who, hearing the word, hold it fast in an honest and generous heart, and bring forth fruit with patience. (Lk 8:15)

The pattern of your life

When people come to me looking for spiritual direction, I try to help them to become aware of their own experience and to trust that it is there that God is guiding them. To help them towards this realisation I ask them to dwell on two questions:

1) What has been happening in their life of late?
I hope that in trying to answer this question, people will discover threads of meaning amid the events of the recent part of their story. They will thus be led to clarify the way they see life at present. How important it is for them to gain this clarity about the meaning of life is the theme of Victor Frankl's famous book, *Man's Search For Meaning*.

2) What do they want out of life at present?
This question is geared towards helping people to get in touch with their deep desires. In other words, the question is meant to help them to get a sense of their priorities and which of these priorities they are now ready to take responsibility for.

The search for *meaning* and *direction* which these two questions are meant to stimulate is a very basic one. The search presupposes that there is a pattern or a design in all your experience and that life is not just all loose ends.

Is there a design in life or is it just loose ends?
I remember an incident which took place when I was working as a missionary in Africa. I was attending an assembly at which a new man was taking over as Provincial or as leader of a big group of missionaries who were involved in a wide variety of activities. It was a time of change and those missionaries were not sure where they were going as a group. So they were asking this new man for some clarification of the direction in which they were meant to be moving.

In an effort to explain where he stood, the Provincial took as an illustration the miniature tapestries which his mother used to make. He explained how she used to weave a design with various colours of wool onto a piece of strong gauze. When she was finished there was a very colourful design woven onto one side of the gauze. On the other side, however, there was a mass of disorganised loose ends.

In answer to their question then, he said that he had to admit that all he could see as he took over his new job was a mass of loose ends. He concluded by saying that he was sure that God saw the other side, with its beautiful design, and that he was convinced that God would help them in time to see something of that side also.

The formless side of the tapestry is what life seems to be like when what happens to us appears to be a series of unconnected events with no apparent pattern or design to them. There is however, in the way our dream unfolds, a very distinct design. Like the dream in the acorn, ours is gradually realised in a constant, consistent and unique way. There are definite patterns which are unique to each of us in the way that God influences our minds and hearts. These patterns keep repeating themselves in a consistent way.

Recurring patterns

There are two aspects of our dream which we examined in Chapter 1 that are very significant here. These are that our deep dream unfolds in a *unique* as well as in a *constant* way. This means that our dream will evolve in a way that is similar to, and consistent with, the way it has developed in previous periods of our life. So there will be *recurring patterns* in the way each of us experiences our dream.

These recurring patterns will manifest themselves in the way we gradually adopt a distinctive vision or outlook which gives our life meaning. These recurring patterns will also appear in what we feel strongly about, in our deep desires and in the distinctive set of priorities which give our life a sense of direction. There is, as a result, a pattern or design in the way we see life, as well as in the way we feel about it. Nobody can tell us this, we must find it for ourselves.

This exercise is meant to arouse the dormant experience of the recurring patterns of enlightenment and attraction which give our lives meaning and direction. We will be trying to heighten our awareness of how God has been active in all of this, moulding our minds and hearts, so that we might accept the gospel of his love and providence.

Yet God (that hews mountain and continent,
Earth, all, out; who, with trickling increment,
Veins violets and tall trees makes more and more)
Could crowd career with conquest while there went
Those years and years by of world without event
That in Majorca Alfonso watched the door.
(G M Hopkins)

THE EXERCISE

1) Express briefly what is the most striking insight into life which has come to you of late. Also record one deep desire or attraction which has become a priority for you. Is there a saying, a line of a song or a phrase from Scripture, which captures for you the insight and the deep desire?

2) Are there other examples of convictions, and of what you consider really worthwhile, which strike you as being distinctly yours? List a couple of examples from such areas of your life as your relationships, your work or your leisure. Are these convictions about what is really true or worthwhile peculiar to this period of your life or have they a history in previous periods? Describe the circumstances when one of these truths or values emerged in your life.

In doing this part of the Exercise, you are trying to notice the unique yet constant patterns of your experience. There will be a consistency as well as a distinct difference about the way you see life and feel about it from one period of it to another. Note too how your vision and your values differ from those of people, like the members of your own family, who were brought up in very similar circumstances to yours.

3) Note what role you feel God has had in the birth and maturing of the vision and the values which are distinctively yours. Use the three steps of reflection, given at the end of Exercise 2, to heighten your awareness of one instance of how God has moulded your mind and heart in some way.

Don't let the world around you squeeze you into its own mould, but let God re-mould your minds from within. (Rom 12:2)

4) Imagine yourself being interviewed about the present period of your life. You are asked to make notes beforehand on the way you would address some key issues in your life. You are asked, for example, whether your outlook has changed, whether you see things differently now from the way you used to. Again, you are asked if your priorities have changed and if you now value some things more and some less than before. Finally, you are asked whether your change of outlook and sense of priorities has affected your lifestyle.

5) It would be very worthwhile to make a synthesis of the ideas and values which govern your life at present. It may help to notice how you react when you are reading an article in a newspaper which expresses strong views. You will find yourself reacting to what is said as you find you agree or disagree with the writer. This is evidence that you have strong convictions about what is true and what is worthwhile.

Begin your personal synthesis by noting some of these convictions which you have about areas of your life such as your relationships, your work, your leisure and the spiritual side of your life. It may help to look at what are the concerns of your average day, or where do you go when you have leisure time. It would be good if you could express your convictions with the help of a diagram. This might take the form of a circle and you could illustrate how important convictions are for you by putting the more deeply held ones closer to the centre of your circle.

6) Imagine yourself invited to visit a wisdom figure. This is a person who for you is a symbol of wisdom, or who helps you to develop a sense of inner clarity about the meaning and purpose of life. So quieten yourself and in your imagination make your way up the mountain to where this wise person lives. It is important to enjoy the atmosphere of freedom and perspective which you get as you ascend. Sit down at some point on your journey and focus on one or two basic issues which you want to talk about to your wisdom figure.

When you meet this person, listen to her answers and to where she takes the conversation. Allow her to be very affirming, i.e. appreciative of all there has been in your life. Let her also affirm you in the sense of wanting what is best for you in the future.

Somewhere on your journey back down the mountain, sit down and write out your impressions of your meeting. As you write, clarify for yourself any insight you got into the meaning and purpose of your life.

7) A fantasy about the tapestry of your life may help you to stay with, and to appreciate, what you have discovered above about the pattern of your life.

Begin the fantasy by quietening yourself. Then imagine that you are in your inner room. This is a place within you where all the important things about your life story are recorded. Look at the pictures and symbols around the walls as illustrating the different seasons of your mind and heart over the years.

Next, let God direct your attention to all of this and then let him invite you to appreciate it, especially the tapestry of your life at the centre of the room. In the rich design and colours of this tapestry is recorded the way God has been weaving 'all things together onto good for you.' (Rom 8:28) Admire the richness of the colours and the pattern. Ask God what these represent and allow yourself to appreciate the goodness of your life which the colours and the design illustrate. Notice particularly the meaning of the rich veins of gold and silver which run through the dark colours. End the fantasy by expressing how you feel. The following verses may help you do this.

> My life is but a weaving
> Between the Lord and me;
> I cannot choose the colours,
> He worketh steadily.
>
> Oft-times he weaveth sorrow,
> And I, in foolish pride
> Forget he sees the upper,
> And I the under side.
>
> Not till the loom is silent
> And the shuttles cease to fly,
> Shall God unroll the canvas
> And explain the reason why.

The dark threads are as needful,
In the weaver's skilful hand,
As the threads of gold and silver
In the pattern he has planned.

He knows, he loves, he cares –
Nothing this truth can dim;
He gives the very best to those
Who leave the choice with him.
(Anonymous)

EXERCISE 4

The story of two selves

In Exercises 1-3 we looked at how we can discover an underground stream of inner wisdom in the recurring patterns of meaning and direction we find in our story. We also looked at the influence of God's providence in the formation of this inner wisdom. We now move on to look at two important aspects of our story which we need to face if our dream is to be fully realised.

The rich and the poor self
We will notice in our story that there are times of light and times of darkness, times when life is meaningful and times when we seem to be walking in a thick fog. We will notice a self who is clear and enthusiastic about life, and another unenthusiastic self for whom life is confusing. Sometimes we notice that we are in touch with, and charged up by, our deep dream's joy in being loved and loving. At other times we notice that we feel flat and indifferent about such things.

In our story, then, two selves emerge. One of these is poor and the other is rich. The poor self is limited and sinful, while the rich self realises that it has brought much of its dream to full flower. Both these selves have constructive roles to play which are essential for the realisation of our dream. We may doubt whether our limitations can be constructive, but the experience of our human poverty is essential for the fullness of life and happiness Jesus wants for us.

Happy are the poor in spirit. (Mt 5:3)

'The shadow is 90% gold'. (Carl Jung)

The constructive and the descructive possibilities of these two selves are symbolised in the story of Rapunzel.

Who do you believe?
There was once a little girl called Rapunzel who was very beau-

EXERCISE 4   53

tiful. She was captured by a witch who knew that if she wanted to hold on to the little girl she had to convince her that she was ugly. If she knew she was beautiful, she would go off with one of the young men who came to consult the witch. If on the other hand, she was convinced she was ugly, she would be afraid of being seen by them, and would therefore hide when they were around. So the witch gradually convinced Rapunzel that she was ugly and she hid for fear of being seen when anyone came to the witch's house.

One day when she was combing her hair in her room, she became conscious of someone looking at her through the window. Instinctively she looked up. It was then that she saw, in the eyes of the young man gazing at her through the window, that she was beautiful. Gradually, as she learned to believe this, her fear was replaced by joy. She set off on the long journey of freeing herself from the deadening influence of the witch in order to accept the life and happiness which the young man's love made available to her.

We have a strong tendency to believe the witch and to accept a very deadening illusion about our deepest self. Even though the weak and wayward side of us is only a small fraction of who we are, we tend to see it as much bigger than it is. The signs of our limitations tend, like a black spot on a sheet of white paper, to fix our attention. The limited side of ourselves can dominate what we see and obscure the vision of ourselves which God wants us to believe in.

For the fascination of evil obscures what is good. (Ws 4:12)

Just as Rapunzel saw her goodness reflected back to her in the young man's eyes, so we are asked to accept what we see in God's eyes. We are asked to believe in the fact that God 'sees and loves in us what he sees and loves in his Son.' (Preface of the Mass) This love of God for us is the ultimate proof that we are supremely worthwhile.

The essential human tragedy

If we accept the witch's exclusive focus on our limited or poor self we get confined to a small corner of life, we take out membership of what John Powell calls the 10% Club. He is convinced, as are most psychologists, that the average person is only 10% alive.

We realise only 10% of our ability to be loved and to be loving. We bring to flower only a fraction of the potential of our dream. The reason why we leave so much of our dream lie dormant is that we do not face, or learn to live with, the reality of our limitations as well as with the rich potential that is ours by nature and by grace. This is the human tragedy which caused Jesus to weep.

> As he came near and saw the city, he wept over it, saying, 'If you, even you, had only recognised on this day the things that make for peace! But now they are hidden from your eye.' (Lk 19:41-42)

Accepting the poor and affirming the rich self

This fourth Exercise highlights the need to spend time befriending these two aspects of ourselves that are essential to the realisation of our dream. In the parable of the weeds among the wheat (Mt 13:24-30) Jesus illustrated the need to live with our limitations as well as with our rich potential. The way to befriend the two is shown in the way Jesus deals with people like the woman in Simon's house. (Lk 7:36-50) He accepts her as she is, without criticism or a word of correction. He also affirms all the good he finds in her as well as expressing his wish for her peace. Jesus' acceptance of our poor self, and his affirmation of our richness, is constantly being repeated in the gospel. It has the effect of releasing the energy of our dream, just as it did in the case of Zacchaeus in Lk 19:1-10.

THE EXERCISE

1) We are a concoction of good and bad, of strength and weakness. What words and images best capture for you these two sides of someone you know well? Take the story of a film or a story which you have read, and notice the struggle between the ideal and less than ideal sides of one character in the story. Do you notice this conflict in yourself? Does Paul's description of this conflict, in Rom 7:14-25, ring true to you?

> For I know that nothing good dwells within me, that is, in my flesh. I can will what is right, but I cannot do it. For I do not do the good I want, but the evil I do not want is what I do. Now if I do what I do not want, it is no longer I that do it, but sin that dwells within me. So I find it to be a law that when I want to do what is good, evil lies close at hand. For I delight in the law of God in my inmost self, but I see in my members another law at

war with the law of my mind, making me captive to the law of sin that dwells in my members. (Rom 7:18-23)

2) Mention some key events in the story of your relationship with your limited and wayward self. Notice how you see this side of yourself. What words or images would you use to express your relationship with this aspect of yourself? What are your feelings about your human limitedness? Go through the same procedure with the aspect of yourself you feel proud of, noting down how you have related, and what images and feelings you associate with your rich human potential.

3) Recall a time when a friend revealed to you his or her weakness or failure. How did you react? Did it make you more sympathetic towards that person? Did it become constructive in the way you related from then on?

4) Is there an element of tragedy about the fact that we are so out of touch with ourselves? Does the fact that we realise only 10% of our potential surprise you? Does any explanation of why we leave so much of our potential unrealised make sense to you? Would the words injustice, impoverishment or dehumanising be too strong to express the tragedy that we realise so little of our dream? What words would you choose yourself to express this human tragedy?

5) After quietening and centring yourself, contemplate Jesus weeping over Jerusalem. Then listen to him express, in the passage from Luke's gospel given in the introduction to this exercise, what makes him feel so sad. How does contemplating this scene make you feel about your relationship with the side of yourself which wants this peace so much? How do you feel about the part of you which refuses to take the trouble to seek the 'things that are for your peace'?

6) Are there situations which bring out the worst in you, or in which the witch dominates your life as she did Rapunzel's? Describe an experience in which you believed in the witch rather than in the young man. When you reflect back on the incident, do you now feel that you let the dark side of yourself get out of proportion? Do you find that the dark kind of experience, symbolised by the black spot on the white sheet of paper, sometimes dominates your attention? Draw a circle and shade in the proportion of

it that appears to you to represent the amount of dark experience in your day.

7) Read the fourth chapter of St John's gospel and ponder the way Jesus is at home with the limited and sinful side of the Samaritan woman. Notice too how Jesus releases the rich potential of her dream so that she leaves him full of enthusiasm. What words would you use to express Jesus' attitude to your poor self as well as to your rich self? Let Jesus speak these words to you and then tell him honestly how you feel.

PART II

Introduction to Exercises 5-10

In the following six exercises we will try to develop a way of facing the dark side of our story. If we are not willing to be at home with the less than ideal self it will block the realisation of our dream. If we are unwilling to descend into the valley periods of life we will not be able to attain its peaks. We will confine ourselves to the flat uneventfulness of life.

Descending into the dark chasm

At the end of his quest for the Holy Grail, Parsifal saw in the distance, the castle where the object of his life-long quest lay. However, as he got nearer the castle he came on a deep chasm that had to be crossed if he was to reach the castle. This abyss was so deep that he could not see the bottom. Even though the beginning of the path into it was clear, the depths it led down into soon became obscure. Parsifal was not sure what awaited him in his descent so he was anxious to avoid its forbidding darkness. He grasped at the possibility that he might find a bridge but, after searching for a long time, he became convinced that there was no way to attain the Grail than this descent into what seemed a bottomless darkness.

The following brief description of the exercises in Part II will give an outline of the path we will follow in our effort to face the dark side of our story in a healthy way.

Exercise 5 seeks to help us face our human limitations, as opposed to avoiding them. Facing our limitations involves noticing, naming and sharing how we feel about this limited side of ourselves. We thus become free from the destructive effects of this aspect of our human poverty and find how constructive it can become.

Exercise 6 seeks to face another side of our human poverty, our sinfulness. We will look at the destructiveness of sin and how we are involved in it. Finally, in looking at how our infidelity can reveal God's faithful love, we may hope to discover some of the joy which Jesus promises to the poor of Spirit.

Exercise 7 examines how our human poverty can be an invitation or a frustration, according as we find meaning in it or not. We will look at various constructive ways of viewing our poverty as well as the destructive ways in which we are prone to interpret it.

Exercise 8 shows us how Exercises 5-7 may help us see our daily experience of darkness in a new light. We will try to become more sensitive and responsive to the tell-tale signs of the witch's illusion in our day

Exercise 9 aims at healing us in the way the two disciples were healed on the road to Emmaus. We let a healthy Jesus invite us to share our desolation with him so that he can put it in perspective for us.

Exercise 10 tells us how to go about a more radical form of healing called *vision therapy*. This involves replacing our distorted vision of ourselves with the vision which Christ invites us to accept.

Facing your limitations

In this Exercise we will become aware of our human limitations as an area of our poverty which we are constantly being invited to face. There is something about these limitations that we are afraid of and therefore refuse to confront.

The beast in the forest
There was once a village in the middle of a forest. The people who lived there were terrified by a beast which they believed lived among the trees that surrounded their homes. They had all heard its fierce roar and some were said to have even seen it. So they lived in fear, hoping that if they ignored it, the beast would go away. When it did not, they hired many hunters to rid them of it, but none of these succeeded in doing so.

Then one day a great warrior came to their village and promised to show them how to rid their lives of the beast. They agreed to pay him well if he should succeed, and so he set off into the forest.

As he sought the beast he, like the villagers, was very afraid, especially when he heard its roar or caught a glimpse of its fearsome appearance. Unlike the villagers, however, he kept on after the beast, in spite of his fear. With each sighting of the beast he noticed a strange thing happening. Every time he caught sight of the beast or heard its roar, it looked smaller and sounded less fearsome.

Eventually when he cornered the beast, he was amazed to see that it had become very small. Before plunging his lance into it, he asked, 'Who are you?' 'My name is *fear*,' replied the beast.

The beast in the forest is a symbol of something in each of us that we are fearful of facing. It is the dark side of ourselves, the Dark Companion, which we have repressed or banished. It is like a scapegoat we have driven into the wilderness. This side of ourselves is something we find hard to face, as it puts us in touch with the fact that we do not control life, that we are by nature limited and destined to die. This reality of our human limitations can generate within us a lot of negative feelings and especially fear.

Because this experience of our limitations is often so painful, we tend to repress or bury it. Like the people who lived in the forest, we have to learn that this is not a realistic solution. Facing the beast is something no one can do for us, we each have to face the reality of our limitations and the fear which these can generate.

A sense of our limitations

Perhaps the most basic sense of our limitations comes with age, when some things become difficult for us to manage. Even though we may try to repress the signs of approaching death, our limitations are a constant reminder of it.

One of the areas where we experience our limitations most is in our human relationships. In these we often experience rejection, indifference and even hostility. We may have difficulty getting on with people, at work or at home. There may be a lack of intimacy in our relationships which can generate loneliness.

We may not live up to certain standards in our outer and inner life and therefore experience ourselves as failures or half-hearted. We may live with a feeling of insignificance and the pain of being reminded of this.

We have a limited capacity to change, to leave the familiar for the unknown, with all the insecurity that involves. Even when we strive to change, we can experience frustration of our long and short term plans.

When we pray we may feel that things are out of our control when we become immersed in distractions and dryness.

O Lord, God of my salvation, when, at night, I cry out in your presence, let my prayer come before you; incline your ear to my cry. For my soul is full of troubles, and my life draws near to Sheol. I am counted among those who go down to the Pit; I am like those who have no help. (Ps 88:1-4)

Out of the depths I cry to you, O Lord; O Lord, hear my voice. (Ps 130)

Facing our limitations

Each of us has to deal with some degree of darkness each day and our happiness will depend a lot on how we handle it. We have to 'take up our cross daily', learning to live with our limitations in a constructive way.

The shadow is 90% gold. This was Carl Jung's way of stating his belief in the constructive possibilities of the less than ideal side of our lives. This less than ideal self can become constructive or 'become gold', if we learn to face it in some way like the following:

1) We need to *notice* the signs of the deadening aspects of our shadow surfacing. These signs take the form of strong negative feelings.

2) We then need to articulate or *name* these feelings.

3) Finally, we need to *share* them with ourselves as we would with another person, in order to accept and even befriend this shadow side of ourselves.

It is hoped that in this way the shadow side of us may become 90% gold.

The fruit of this kind of awareness is freedom from being dominated and deadened by our human limitations, and the negative feelings which arise from them. Our hope for this liberation is based on a principle that states: To become aware of our negative feelings is to control them; not to become aware, is to be controlled by them. To name the demon is to slay it.

One of the reasons why people are reluctant to face the beast in the forest, or the shadow side of themselves, is that this may involve arousing very painful experiences. Therefore, as you go through the exercise that follows, it is important to begin with less traumatic experiences or with a small portion of the more painful ones. It is easy to find ourselves overwhelmed when we suddenly release an accumulation of strong negative feeling. If we have not been used to releasing it in an ongoing way, it can become like the excessive build up of water behind the dam wall. We need to develop a way of releasing it very gently and gradually.

THE EXERCISE

1) What kinds of situations get you down or bother you most? What areas of your life cause you difficulty, hardship or darkness? Where in general do you experience your limitations most keenly?

2) How do you react to the experience of your limitations? Name some of the negative feelings or unhealthy dark moods that tend to dominate your life as a result of being faced with your shadow. Do you tend to project the blame for your moods on to others?

3) Take one incident where you have experienced your limitations, and re-live it. You may need to prepare for this by asking yourself questions like the following and then noting down what you find:

What happened that caused such strong negative feeling? How did you interpret the meaning of what happened? Are there images that you associate with this experience?

4) Make a list of the kinds of hardship you have come up against in the present period of your life. Recall what happened, what you felt and images you associate with the experience. Next, do the same for the period that preceded the present one, and so on, until you have a sense of your 'dark history'.

5) Staying with the dark side of your story, make a list of the kinds of hardship or difficulty that recur. Then list the kind of negative feelings or dark moods you associate with these valley periods of your life. When you have finished, note down how you feel. For example, do you feel a greater understanding and compassion for yourself, and less inclination to bolt the door against this dark side of yourself? Do you feel any of the peace, contentment or joy that Jesus says belongs to the 'poor in spirit'?

6) Make a rough diagram for yourself, using a number of circles, one inside the other. Put the kinds of hardship you find most difficult to handle closest to the centre. When you have finished, be with this very vulnerable side of yourself as you would be with a friend who has revealed to you an area of weakness.

7) Describe how you now see and how you feel about your limitations and your less than ideal self as a result of doing this exercise. Next, imagine yourself sitting beside your dark companion. See

what you want to say to your dark companion and then what your dark companion wants to say to you in reply. Carry on with this dialogue until both sides have said all they want to. Finally spend time with how you feel towards each other as a result of talking heart to heart.

Your sinful self

The Grail Legend is a striking symbol of the essential human quest. The fact that we get side-tracked or seduced by something other than this object of our deepest searching, is another theme of the legend, and the one we will focus on in this exercise. The result of this seduction may not appear to be very serious, but it can mean the loss of the love which is the object of our dream. It is important that we face the reality of this disaster. As you read the following version of the Grail Legend, notice how it portrays this tragedy.

The Grail Legend
The Holy Grail is the chalice and platter used by Christ at the Last Supper. It is kept in a castle whose king is unaware of its presence. The king is, as a result, afflicted by a debilitating illness which nobody can heal. His whole kingdom shares the effects of his sickness and lies desolate.

In a remote part of the kingdom, there lives a simple, naïve youth called Parsifal. On being trained as a knight he is given three rules to live by. The first two are that he must not seduce or be seduced, and the third is that he must seek the Holy Grail and an answer to the question, 'Whom does the Grail serve?'

With these instructions in mind Parsiful sets off to look for the Holy Grail.

After many years on his journey, he eventually meets the king who invites him to his castle. When Parsifal fails to recognise the Holy Grail and to ask the crucial question, his visit to the castle is fruitless. The king is not healed and the land continues to be desolate. So Parsifal has to set out on his journey again. He gets seduced by many things and diverted from his quest until after many wanderings he forgets all about the Holy Grail.

Eventually he meets a hermit who absolves him and who gives him instructions on how to find the Grail castle. When he finds it, he asks the vital question and receives the answer:

The Grail must serve the Grail King.

As a result of becoming aware, with Parsifal's help, of the Holy Grail and the need to devote himself to serving the One it represented, the king is healed. He and his kingdom are cured and their desolation gives way to joy as they learn to acknowledge the presence of the Holy Grail.

The nature of sin and its destructiveness

One of the very striking things about the Grail legend is the profound understanding of our sinfulness which it expresses. It highlights a concept of sin as being seduced and getting cut off from the love of God and others. Here are some of the ways the Scripture portrays this concept of sin:

1) Sin means drifting out of relationship with God, oneself and others. This tendency to drift manifests itself in our unwillingness to take the time to establish intimate relationships and to maintain them by the necessary communication. (Lk 15:11-32, Lk 10:38-42)

2) Sin means being unfaithful to the true God because we chase after false ones. In other words, we are seduced by superficial desires and as a result miss the one thing necessary. (Hos 2, Ezk 16, Lk 12:16-21, Lk 8:14)

3) Sin means becoming separated from God, from our deeper selves and from others. When we thus get cut off from our essential relationships we become lonely, sad and dehumanised. By our making something superficial all-important, the 'one thing necessary' becomes secondary. (Gn 3:1-24 & 4:1-16, Rom 1:16-32)

4) Sin means believing the witch, rather than God, and thus becoming prisoners of the dark 10% of life. We become impoverished by neglecting the 90% that is life-giving. We fail to believe the Good News and to appreciate and be grateful for the large proportion of life that is really good. (Lk 14:16-24, Rev 3:16-32)

How does God react to sin?

Even more important than our involvement in something so destructive as sin, is the way God reacts to this destructiveness. If it is seen apart from God's fidelity, our waywardness and the way it dehumanises us, becomes a depressing picture. It is only against the background of God's fidelity to us that our infidelity can be seen in a constructive way.

Father, how wonderful your care for us! How boundless your merciful love! To ransom a slave you gave away your Son. O happy fault, O necessary sin of Adam which gained for us so great a redeemer! (*The Exultet*)

In the Exodus, the Israelites had a profound experience of how God's love endured in spite of their infidelity. The following verses are the conclusion they came to at the end of their journey in the desert; they discovered God's fidelity in their own infidelity.

The Lord, the Lord, a God merciful and gracious, slow to anger and abounding in steadfast love and faithfulness, keeping steadfast love for thousands, forgiving iniquity and transgression and sin, but who will by no means clear the guilty. (Ex 34:6-7)

When God says he does not 'clear the guilty', it means that he does not throw a blanket over our sinfulness and its destructiveness. He never disguises the horror of what sin does to us. However, if we are willing to struggle to return to him, he will, like the father of the Prodigal Son, come running to welcome us back.

But while he was yet at a distance his father saw him and had compassion, he ran and embraced him and kissed him. (Lk 15:20)

Yet even now, says the Lord, return to me with all your heart, with fasting, with weeping and with mourning; and rend your hearts and not your garments. Return to the lord your God for he is gracious and merciful, slow to anger and abounding in steadfast love. (Joel 2:12-13)

Other places where God's reaction to our sinfulness is expressed are: Lk 15:20-24, 28, Ho 2:14-23, Lk 7:36-50, Lk 19:1-10

In this Exercise, we seek to face the poverty created by our sinfulness. We do this in the belief that a lot of our happiness lies in our being at home with, and even befriending, our wayward self, in the way that God does. This belief is at the heart of the Beatitudes that are so central to the gospel.

Happy are the poor in spirit for theirs is the kingdom of God.
(Mt 5:3)

The aim of this exercise, then, is to face our poverty in a constructive way, in a way that will be healing and life-giving. We will seek to do this by heightening our awareness of,
a) How dehumanising and destructive our sinfulness is.
b) How we are personally involved in something so destructive.
c) How God accepts and is at home with us as sinners, while wanting us to face the human impoverishment of sin.

THE EXERCISE

1) Make a list of the worst things that you find happening in the world today. Are some of these things more tragic or destructive than others? Describe one in some detail. How do you feel about what it is doing to the people involved?

Are there words or images which depict for you what is seriously wrong about all these happenings? Would you find echoes of your own wrongdoing in these words and images? Do you find yourself involved in the evil that is going on around you? If you do, try to put words on how you see yourself as part of it.

2) Which understanding of sin, given on page 67, do you identify with? What way does this understanding of sin differ from the one you had in the past? Take an example of a time when you sinned and look at your sin in the light of the way you now understand it. Read one of the scripture passages on page 67 which are associated with your way of understanding sin.

3) Take some examples of your sinfulness in the present period of your life and note down what you see to be unhealthy or even destructive about them. Would you find the word 'destructive' a bit strong to describe the way you see and feel about these experiences of your sinfulness? What words would you find more suitable to describe the wrong you have done and how you feel about being involved in this? Would words like tragic, horrific, disgusting, dehumanising, impoverishing or unjust be too mild, or would they be adequate, or too strong?

4) We need to develop a sense of our dark history. This is the story of the unique and recurring pattern of sin in each person's life. Begin to do this by moving back through the various stages of your life. With each stage, note down the ways you got side-tracked,

the ways you understood and felt about this waywardness at the time. Are there images or lines of Scripture that would capture what these experiences meant to you at the time and what they mean to you now?

5) What kind of relationship do you have with your dark companion, with the wayward self of your dark history? What way do you look on this side of yourself? Do you feel sympathetic, sensitive and accepting, or out of touch, lacking in understanding and intolerant? Would you like to befriend this part of yourself more in the future?

Is it true to say that we love the poor outside us in the same way that we love the poor person inside us?

6) After quietening and centring yourself, begin a dialogue with your dark companion. Give your dark companion and yourself a chance to speak. Write down as you go along what each of you says. Let the two of you say how you see things and express how you feel about each other. Let each of you say how you would like to see things work out between you in the future, and what you each want to do about this. When you finish the dialogue, read back through it, and see how you feel.

Your poverty:
invitation or frustration ?

There is a crucial choice we have to make, which was highlighted in Exercises 5 and 6. It is crucial because on it depends whether the experience of our poverty becomes an invitation or a frustration.

St Bruno and the Bullfrog

The Prayer of St Bruno was interrupted by the croaking of the bullfrog. When he could stand it no longer, he shouted out the window, 'Would you, please, be quiet! I am trying to pray.' So all went quiet and Bruno settled down to pray. However, a voice inside him kept insisting, 'Perhaps the frog was praying too, and God may be as pleased with its prayer as with yours'.

When he could gainsay the voice no longer, Bruno ordered all the frogs to sing. From then on he was no longer distracted by the song of the bullfrog, for he had learned not to fight the prayer of creation but to be in harmony with it. A whole new world of prayer then opened up for Bruno.

Bruno was upset by the frog, as long as he was seeing what it was doing as interrupting him at his prayer. When, however, he was led to see what the frog was doing as what it was made for, the whole picture changed. What was a disturbing noise became the prayer of the frog, and what was a frustration became an invitation to join the frog in praise of its creator. There is a fundamental principle involved here which will be central to this exercise. It states that it is not people or circumstances which upset us, but the way we decide to interpret or think about them.

This exercise is meant to help us understand how the experience of our weak and wayward selves can be an invitation to grow. The darkness which the experience of our limitations and sinfulness causes need not necessarily be a frustration. The shadow can, as Jung believed, become 90% gold. However, it does not just happen. There is a difficult choice involved, if our limitations are to be a source of growth, if they are to lead to 'life' rather than to 'death'.

> I set before you life or death, blessing or curse. Choose life, then, so that you and your descendants may live in the love of the Lord your God, obeying his voice, clinging to him; for in this your life consists. (Deut 30:29-30)

The same situation can be for one person inspiring and enlivening, where for another it can be depressing and deadening. It is amazing how differently two people can see the same situation and how differently they are affected by what they see.

> Two men looked out through prison bars
> one saw the mud, the other the stars

A choice of two ways

The way we choose to interpret the poverty we have noticed in the last two exercises, will determine the way we go, whether towards 'life' or 'death'. As we have already seen it is not the events or the people in our lives that enliven or deaden us, but the way we think about them.

Two Interpretations

1) If we see life in the context of what the witch is saying, which is that we are insignificant, much of what we experience will confirm us in this conviction of our insignificance. This illusion is a very painful experience, so it causes a lot of strong negative feeling such as guilt, fear or frustration.

2) Life, however, can also be seen in the context of faith. From this point of view, our poverty can arouse and challenge our conviction that we are the object of God's love and providence. Thus our weakness and waywardness can generate very positive feelings of the joy which follows faith, the conviction that we are loved and lovable, no matter what.

There are, as we saw in the story of Rapunzel, two ways of interpreting our experience. One of these interpretations, that of the witch, leads to the paralysing fear of being seen as ugly. The other interpretation, that of the young man looking at us through the window, is an invitation to a way of seeing things that enlivens us and makes us happy. We are responsible for which of these two images of ourselves we choose and thus for the consolation or desolation that inevitably follow our choice. Like Cain, we are responsible for mastering our tendency to drift down into desolation, for not allowing ourselves to be devoured by it.

God asked Cain, 'Why are you angry and downcast? If you are well disposed, ought you not to lift up your head? But if you are ill disposed, is not sin at the door like a crouching beast hungering for you, which you must master?' (Gn 4:6-7)

We have seen, in general terms, how our experience of our limitations can make us, as it did St Bruno, content or discontent. We will look first at how this experience can make us discontent or even desolate and lead us down the road to 'destruction.' (Mt 7:13-14)

Our poverty as destructive

There are three levels of discontent or desolation which we will notice ourselves at times drifting into. At each level it will not be people or circumstances which cause the desolation but the way we interpret what is happening to us. The telltale sign of the fact that we are misinterpreting a situation or that we are suffering from some illusion is a prolonged and excessive feeling of discontent or upset.

Three levels of illusion and desolation

1) The first level of discontent is brought on by the illusion that something we say in anger, for example, is allowed to colour unduly the way we see our day. So if we get frustrated, all we may see at the end of the day is this disturbing 5% which, like a small black spot, dominates our attention.

2) The second level of discontent or desolation emerges when we let some recurring negative feeling dominate the way we see ourselves. We can easily identify with the ugly mood we repeatedly find ourselves in. This mood, like the black spot on the sheet of white paper, fixes our attention and becomes all we see. On reflection, this way of interpreting our experience can be seen to be an illusion. Our ugly mood is only a small fraction of the kind of person we are.

3) The third level of desolation is the most destructive, for here our poor self image resists or blocks our belief in the Good News that we are wholly and deeply loved by God. Nothing God says to us about his love can gainsay the deeply ingrained convictions about our lack of worth which we hold on to so tightly.

Our poverty as constructive

The experience of our human poverty, manifest in our limitations and sinfulness, can also become a healthy one. For it to become so, however, we have to learn to see or interpret this experience of our poverty in some way like one of the following.

1) The experience of our human limitations and waywardness can lead to the *poverty of spirit* which Jesus tells us is a source of joy. Rather than putting us in touch with our insignificance, an experience of failure, for example, can confront us with the reality that we do not always control our lives. If we let life's harsh realities put us in touch with a healthy sense of our poverty, we become more open to God's providence.

2) The realisation of our human poverty can also help generate hope in us. It makes us realise that we cannot rely solely on our own resources to get us across life's desert. A sense of our limitations makes room for *hope or trust in God* and in his promises to lead us to the Promised Land.

3) Life's hardships challenge our *faith* with the question, 'Do you really believe in God's love and providence? Like Thomas, we tend to accept as real only what we feel. So we say, 'If I feel God cares for me, it is real; if I don't, it is not.' The essential of faith, however, is the conviction of things not seen. (Heb 11:1) Our poverty can help us make the leap from feeling God's love, to the conviction that it is real. This is in spite of what our feelings may be saying.

4) The full strength of God's loving-kind and faithful *love* is often revealed only against the background of our own lack of love and fidelity. This experience invites us to see ourselves loved in spite of our infidelity. If the prodigal son in us never owns up to the extent of our poverty, we will not realise the extent and the intensity of the Father's love of us.

THE EXERCISE

1) A lot of writers today talk about the significance of strong negative feelings. Does this belief of theirs, that this kind of feeling is saying a lot to us, mean much to you? After quietening yourself, become aware of a typical situation where you are inclined to get upset and which gives rise to negative feelings. Use words, phrases or images to describe the situation, how it made you feel and how you understand or interpret what was going on.

2) List some situations which you find difficult to handle and then list the typical negative feelings you associate with each of these situations. Does the principle which says that it is not people or circumstances which upset us but the way we interpret what is happening, make sense to you? What ways do you see yourself misinterpreting the difficult situations of your life?

List as many of the negative feelings as you can which you experience in the valley periods of your life. Do many of these negative feelings rule your day by causing you to be in a bad mood? When you feel negative or in a bad mood, is this telling you something about how you see the situation? Are you inclined to blame people or events when you feel bad, or do you own the fact that it has to do with the way you interpret what is happening?

3) What way do you experience the witch saying to you, 'You are ugly?' Is it, for example, coming across to you as a feeling of insignificance, a feeling that arises from not being commended much? Use words, phrases or images to record the more typical versions of the witch's message you identify with or believe in. What kind is the poor self image that the witch reflects back to you? What kinds of negative feeling does your experience of inadequacy give rise to in you?

4) Are there ways that you notice yourself getting caught in the trap of the third illusion and the desolation which it generates? What is it about yourself which resists or even rejects the love which your friends, and especially God, want you to accept?

Love, or feeling affirmed and worthwhile, is such a major part of our dream that we must try to earn it if we do not accept it as Grace or as a gift of God. A very difficult question to answer, but one worth asking yourself, is, 'What way of earning love do I employ?'

5) The following are some ways of interpreting the valley periods of your life in a healthy way. Select one of them which you would like to work with and write out a longer version of it that would help you to interpret the difficult patches of your journey:

a) Difficult experiences can help you face the reality of your own limitations and sinfulness. Jesus says there is a special joy in facing this kind of poverty. b) Dark times can stretch and strengthen your faith in God's love and providence. c) You are invited by the

experience of your own poverty to trust in God rather than relying solely on your own resources. d) Many people judge love to
be real only when it is felt. Life's hardship deprives us of that feeling and encourages us to move on to a love that is based on the
conviction of the other person's love.

6) In the light of the exercise so far, write down any reflections
you have on Deut 30:29-30, quoted on page 72, and on the parable
of the two ways in Mt 7:13-14. Describe what the story of Bruno
and the bullfrog, and the saying about the two men looking out
through prison bars, mean to you?

7) Write down any reflection you may have on Jung's statement
that the shadow is 90% gold. Do you think this was borne out for
Bruno when he learned to listen to the song of the frog?

The daily awareness
of your poverty

There is a saying that to name the demon is to slay him. In other words, to become aware of what is making us depressed or desolate is to go a long way towards freeing ourselves from its negative effects. So, the practical concern of this exercise is to become more adept at naming the demon in our daily experience. In attempting to do this, we try to apply what we have learned from Exercises 5-7, to the concrete situations of each day.

A basic human tragedy
We are easily controlled by the voice of our insignificance. This is the illusion that we fall victim to when a small, dark fraction of our lives, becomes the whole picture we see of ourselves. This illusion makes it very difficult for us to accept the gospel vision of God as love and especially ourselves as lovable in his eyes.

Cyrano de Bergerac
Cyrano de Bergerac was a man with an unusually large nose and this became the dominant feature of the way he saw himself. So he could not accept the love of Roxanne, which he craved for, because of this slight disfigurement of an otherwise very noble person. At the end of the story, when Roxanne has developed a profound love for Cyrano, one feels like saying to him, 'Would you forget about your nose and accept her love, and all the life and happiness that it will bring you.' However, Cyrano cannot believe in her love and so he dies, a very sad and lonely man.

Who is leading you and where?
It is our basic tragedy that we believe other voices rather than that of Jesus. Like Cyrano de Bergerac, we succumb to the illusion of our insignificance and thus we take the way to 'destruction'. It is vital that we learn to take the narrow and more difficult road to 'life' by cultivating our belief in the way Jesus sees us.

Enter by the narrow gate; for the gate is wide and the way is easy, that leads to destruction, and those who enter it are many. For the gate is narrow and the way is hard that leads to life, and those who find it are few. (Mt 7:13-14)

To avoid this tragedy of drifting down the road to destruction, it is vital that we develop an ability to become more sensitive and responsive to whether it is Christ or the witch who is leading us. It is easy to be under the influence of the witch, and not to notice where we are being led. Not to discern and heed the warning signs of this, means that we can easily drift down this way to 'destruction'.

Reflection is the opposite of drifting. When we reflect we learn to 1) notice strong negative feelings, 2) discern what these are saying to us about the destructive illusions we live with, and then 3) respond to these negative feelings in a realistic way. Our need to be vigilant and to understand what is going on, in and around us, is a theme Jesus often returns to in sayings like:

Keep your eyes open! Be on your guard against the 'yeast' of the Pharisees (i.e. their blindness) ... Don't you understand or grasp what I say even yet? Are you like the people who having eyes, do not see, and having ears, do not hear? ... And when there were seven loaves for four thousand people, how many baskets of pieces did you pick up? 'Seven', they said. Do you not yet understand, he said. (Mk 8:15-21)

Watching for tell-tale signs

Strong negative feelings are the telltale signs of being on the 'road to destruction'. We might notice, for example, that there is a lot of fear around, connected with an event coming up. We may not want to deal with it, because to do so may appear like opening the floodgates to a lot of painful experience. Leaving it lie beneath the surface however has a deadening effect.

So we get insights from our daily experience if we pay attention to our feelings and what they are saying to us. Small things can have a disproportionate effect, like when we get angry about what may appear to others as quite trivial. It is not trivial for us as it may put us in touch with a destructive body of anger which we have allowed to accumulate.

Understanding these tell-tale signs

The effect of this strong feeling may be that we graduate down through the three levels of illusion, which we looked at in Exercise 7, and end up in a very unhealthy frame of mind. Initially we are thrown by our negative feelings and cannot see much else. These feelings keep disrupting our peace of mind unless we do something about them. If we do not get into perspective what for us corresponds to de Bergerac's nose, it can become what we see in ourselves. We can eventually identify with our poor self image rather than with the one God reflects back to us.

Our most basic tragedy is unbelief. Through it we get cut off from the life-giving effects of God's love because our poor self-image resists or denies that we are lovable. We become prisoners of the dark side of ourselves. This is something we easily drift into, unless we learn how to listen and respond to its beginnings in our daily experience.

The aim of this exercise is to develop a growing capacity to be sensitive and responsive to the two ways which are always opening up to us in our daily experience. Here we focus especially on discerning the signs of our taking the 'road to destruction.' (Mt 7:14)

THE EXERCISE

1) Begin with a prayer for light. This could be like that of Solomon in 1 Kings 3: 5-14, where he asks for a discerning heart. The form you give this opening prayer will gradually emerge as you come to appreciate the importance of God's guidance.

2) Notice any strong negative feeling that arose during the day. This is the telltale sign of something important going on. Walk around in this experience, noticing and putting words on what happened and on how you felt. If no strong negative feeling calls for attention in today's experience, return to a recent occurrence of it.

3) Spend time trying to understand the significance of the strong negative feeling you have noticed. For example, this feeling will tell you who is leading you and where you are being led; along the road to 'life' or down the one to 'destruction'. So in this part of the exercise, spend time cultivating the realisation that the strong negative feelings which recur in your life are not a healthy influence. To recognise something as unhealthy, is to begin to move away from it. In this sense to name the demon is to slay it.

Become more aware of how minor incidents during the day are putting you in touch with a large body of negative feeling from the past. Note how this is affecting you. The feelings which make you desolate may, like the iceberg, be well below the surface, so that you do not notice their presence or their potential for destruction.

There may be a more specific message in your dark feelings and moods. Your fears may be pointing to ways you are misunderstanding the intentions of others, attributing to them a hostility that you are reading into their actions. Awareness of the dark influences at work in your day goes a good way to limiting their influence. Interpreting their meaning, and responding to them fully, will generally require the help of Exercises 9 and 10.

4) When you have noticed yourself being captured by negative feelings and moods, it would help to learn how to share this experience. This sharing can be done with yourself, by writing out how you feel, very sketchily and spontaneously. You are thus preparing yourself for the very important kind of prayer where you share your darkness with God. It is important that you allow yourself to be listened to when you share your darkness, and not to be offered advice. It is very healthy to be listened to, whereas, the last thing you may need is advice.

5) Sometimes the meaning of your day's darkness is clear, so that there is an obvious call to repentance involved. For example you might be aware that your fear is a sign of unbelief in God's providence, in a certain area of your life. In this situation, giving expression to your prayerful desire to change is a good conclusion to this exercise.

Healing Life's Hurts

There is great truth in the saying that a trouble shared is a trouble halved. This is especially true if the person who listens to our troubles is both willing to let us talk and is able to accept and affirm us in what we are going through. Sometimes people are so anxious to lift us out of our problems that they do not allow us the time we need to work our own way through our difficulties. In her book, *On Death And Dying*, Kubler Ross tells us that by giving people advice when they share their experience of being deeply hurt, we can slow down the healing process rather than help it along. We are all like Ivar in the following story, we need to be listened to in a positive or sympathetic way if we are to be healed of life's hurts.

Talking things out
Ivar was a Norwegian poet who was employed by a Swedish king and was prized by him for his skill as a poet, but more so as a counsellor. Ivar was engaged to be married but lost his intended wife when she fell in love with and married his brother. Ivar became desolate and lost all his inspiration as a poet and was too depressed to offer anyone his counsel. The king searched everywhere for a cure but nothing seemed to work. So he was reduced to sitting with Ivar and listening to his troubles each day. To everyone's surprise, the poet broke free of his depression, fell in love again and regained his original inspiration.

There is great virtue in talking things out. Its virtue, however, depends on the honesty with which we are willing to communicate.

When feelings are very strong, affective prayer is possible, only if the person can put them before the Lord and let him accept them. Otherwise, the unnoticed negative feelings will stand like a ridge between him and the Holy One. (*The Practice of Spiritual Direction*, Connolly and Barry)

The Emmaus road experience

This exercise is based on the way Jesus helped two troubled people, on the road to Emmaus. (Lk 24:13-35) By leading them to share their troubles with him and to see these in a new way, Jesus transformed their sorrow into joy. Then, instead of their darkness being a frustration of all they had hoped for, it became a source of a deeper happiness.

Jesus could easily have passed them by knowing the burden of depression they would lay on him. However, he wanted to be with them, to draw out and share their pain. It was in seeing all this in the light of his love of them in the 'breaking of bread', that their sorrow was changed into joy.

> ... your sorrow will be turned into joy. When a woman is in labour she knows pain when her time comes. But when she has given birth she no longer remembers the pain for joy that a child has been born. Now you are going through pain, but I will see you again and your heart will rejoice, and your joy no one will take from you. (Jn 16:21-22)

Being accepted and affirmed

Another typical example of Jesus's reaction to human poverty is the way he deals with the woman in Simon's house. (Lk 7:36-50) There is no sign of criticism, or that Jesus goes along with his host's disapproval of her. Jesus accepts and appreciates her gesture, rather than rejects it. What is most striking in this story, however, is the good he finds and appreciates in her. Where others only saw her poverty, he has an eye for her richness and draws attention to it. She must have left Simon's house, already enjoying the 'peace' or happiness which was his parting wish for her.

> Therefore, I tell you, her sins, which are many, are forgiven, for she loved much; but he who is forgiven little loves little. ... And he said to the woman, 'Your faith has saved you; go in peace.' (Lk 7:47-50)

Jesus' desire to heal us

This exercise assumes that Jesus wants to join us on our way, to listen to and accept our limitations, as well as to express his belief in our goodness. In other words, he wants to do for each of us what he did for the two on the road to Emmaus and for the woman in Simon's house.

By inviting us to believe in the way he sees us Jesus seeks to heal our self-inflicted wounds of unbelief. He also seeks to free us from the desolation which results from our unbelief, to free us from the ways we have become prisoners of the dark side of ourselves.

> 'Lord, if you want to you can make me clean'. Jesus stretched out his hand and placed it on the leper saying, 'Of course I want to, be clean!' (Lk 5:12-13)

> The Spirit of the Lord is upon me, because he has anointed me to bring good news to the poor. He has sent me to proclaim release to the captives and recovery of sight to the blind, to let the oppressed go free, (Lk 4:18)

For this kind of healing to happen, however, we have to share with Jesus as honestly as we can, that area of our life where we are struggling with our weakness and waywardness. We have then to let Jesus put it in the context of his acceptance and appreciation of us. We need to surrender to the mystery that Jesus loves us most where we love ourselves least.

This exercise will follow the steps used by Jesus to lead the two people on the road to Emmaus to regain their enthusiasm for life. We should notice that, in the first part of this encounter, Jesus listens, where in the second part he responds very positively to what they have shared with him.

The *aim* of the Exercise is to *heal* the wounds of our unbelief, and the lack of self-acceptance this involves. It also seeks to *free* us from being dominated by our ugly moods, and the poor self image these tend to generate and sustain. It will help to heal life's hurts and to free us from being dominated by the strong negative feelings they give rise to.

THE EXERCISE

There are four stages of the exercise. You may need to prepare for the second and fourth of these by journaling about:

a) The area of your life where you now want to be healed. You need to decide how much of this woundedness you want to open up. There is always a danger of getting overwhelmed by painful experience from the past, if you open it up all at once. So it is wise to take out only what you can easily handle. Otherwise, you may be so pained at this stage of the exercise that you may not want to go any further.

---

b) You may also need to express in writing what you would be willing to let Jesus say, in appreciation of how good you are in the areas of your life where you are struggling. This is likely to be where you are most heroic, although it may not be at all obvious to you. So you will need to explore the ways in which you are often most admirable where you are struggling with weakness. This exploration is very necessary if you are to be able to let Jesus say it, and to take in and savour what he says.

1) Imagine yourself to be in some quiet place, where you like to be alone, or with a friend. Savour the atmosphere of this place for a while, and then become conscious of Jesus being with you as a *friend*. He really wants to be with you and is not put off by the fact that you do not feel that you are good company just now.

2) Jesus asks if there is any area of darkness that you would like to share with him, anything that is bothering you just now. He says that you often share his passion, and that he would now like to be with you in yours. He listens attentively, and without interrupting, as you share with him what you feel comfortable putting out before him.

3) You may be surprised that Jesus has not interrupted you with the odd comment or piece of advice. However you are anxious to know how he reacts, so you ask him how he feels about what you have said.

Rather than wanting to change you, he accepts you where you are and understands how you feel. He tells you that he knows exactly what is going on in you, for he has often travelled the road you are on.

> For it is not as if we had a high priest who was incapable of feeling our weaknesses with us; but we have one who has been tempted in every way as we are. (Heb 4:15)

Dwell with this acceptance and then see whether you accept and forgive yourself in the way that Jesus accepts and forgives you.

4) Jesus then says he wants you to know how much he *appreciates* how good you are, especially in this area of your life where you feel weak and inadequate. He expresses his *gratitude* to you for all you have done for him, and most of all for the way that you struggle with your weakness. He says that he would like you to ponder the reality that he loves you most where you love yourself least.

FOLLOW YOUR DREAM

Vision therapy

In Exercise 9 the focus was on healing wounds which strong negative feelings like fear can inflict on us. In the first part of the exercise we sought freedom from the deadening effects of being dominated by these feelings. In the second part we sought the healing
power of Jesus' acceptance and affirmation, the healing power of
the vision of ourselves we see in Jesus' eyes. There is an extraordinary statement about the healing power of this kind of faith vision,
or religious outlook, that arrests my attention every time I read it.
Behind it lies a lifetime's experience of one of the most profound
minds of the twentieth century.

The most radical kind of healing
Among all my patients in the second half of life – that is to say
over thirty five – there has not been one whose problem in the
last resort was not that of finding a religious outlook on life. It
is safe to say that every one of them fell ill because he had lost
what the living religions of every age have given to their fol-
lowers, and none of them has really been healed who did not
regain his religious outlook. (Carl Jung)

This kind of healing is, in a general sense, vision therapy.
Through it we seek a radical form of healing by seeing what has
happened to us, in the light of our faith in Jesus. We seek to replace
the unhealthy or distorted vision of the witch with the one that we
see reflected back to us from Christ's eyes. We replace the illusion
of our insignificance with the reality that, for Jesus, we are supremely worthwhile.

It's the vision that counts
Letting go of our distorted vision, or our false images of ourselves
and God, is basic to the gospel's call to repent and believe. In the
past we have associated repentance mainly with a change of behaviour. In fact repentance involves letting go of our illusions. These

restrict or block our belief in the vision that faith puts before us. The illusion of unbelief inflicts on us the most deadly wound, for by our unbelief we get cut off from what is essentially life-giving, i.e. our faith in God's love and providence.

> To remind them of your oracles they were bitten, and then were quickly delivered, so that they would not fall into deep forgetfulness and become unresponsive to your kindness. For neither herb nor poultice cured them, but it was your word, O Lord, that heals all people. For you have power over life and death; you lead mortals down to the gates of Hades and back again. (Wis 16:11-13)

When people get cut off from God's love by their 'deep forgetfulness', they live in a cold and hostile world where they have to earn their own worth. When they thus try to earn their worth, rather than accepting it as given by faith, they easily become victims of the witch who confirms them in their worthlessness. This wound of worthlessness, brought on by our unbelief, is the most deadly of all. There are different degrees in our woundedness brought on by three levels of illusion we are prone to. The three are described on page 73 but here is an outline of them:

Three basic illusions

1) There is first of all our tendency to let what is negative about a small fraction of our day colour all that we see.

2) A deeper and more damaging illusion, is where we let the 5% of life that is a mess, and that makes us desolate, dominate the way we see ourselves and the way we feel.

3) The most wounding illusion is created by not facing the reality that our worth is a given. It is part of the Good News that God is loving and we are lovable and supremely worthwhile in his eyes.

> You were adorned with gold and silver, while your clothing was of fine linen, rich fabric, and embroidered cloth. You had choice flour and honey and oil for food. You grew exceedingly beautiful, fit to be a queen. Your fame spread among the nations on account of your beauty, for it was perfect because of my splendour that I had bestowed on you, says the Lord God. (Ezek 16:13-14)

This illusion of unbelief is the one that wounds us most deeply, just as it is faith or belief that heals us and makes us fully alive again. To the woman with a haemorrhage, who touched him in the belief that she would be cured, Jesus said, 'Daughter, your faith has made you well; go in peace.' (Lk 8:48)

A radical change of mind and heart

Vision therapy involves a radical change of mind and heart. This change is very difficult because our prejudices have become deeply ingrained over the years. The importance of our ability to change in this radical way is strikingly put by William James in his *Principles of Psychology:*

> Man alone of all the creatures of the earth can change his own pattern. Man alone is the architect of his destiny. The greatest discovery of our generation is that human beings, by changing the inner attitudes of their minds, can change the outer aspects of their lives.

The primary thing we have to change then, is 'the inner attitude of our minds', or what Jung called, our 'religious outlook'. For it is our vision that is the source of the way we feel, and this in turn controls the way we act. It is our way of seeing things that determines the way we feel and the way we act. This is the reason why vision therapy is the most radical kind of healing.

Stages of vision therapy

A full explanation of all that is involved in this form of therapy is given in John Powell's book, *Fully Human and Fully Alive.* He bases his understanding of vision therapy on the principle that it is not people or circumstances that cause us strong negative feeling, but the way we think about these.

Strong negative feelings are a sign of where we are living with an illusion or with a distorted vision of things. Vision therapy aims at searching for the specific illusions, or distorted vision, that are the root cause of the negative feelings which deaden our lives. These feelings, then, will be the telltale sign of where our vision is unhealthy. If, for example, we are fearful, it is usually a sign that we do not see God as provident in the area of life where we feel this way.

Once we have noticed this kind of strong negative feeling we have to find what illusion, or distorted way of seeing things, is causing it. When we find this we have to set about replacing it. From then on, every time we notice the negative feeling surfacing, we have to assert the right way of seeing things. Eventually it is hoped that the correct vision will replace the distorted one. We will thus cut the roots of those feelings that are causing us to be desolate because they restrict or block our belief in the way God sees us.

Take for example the depressing feelings we have if we accept the fact of our insignificance or the witch's vision of ourselves as 'ugly'. Once we notice what is causing us to feel badly, we have to be ready with some simple way of asserting our significance in God's eyes, that he loves us as he does Jesus. We might use words like the following in the form of a mantra: '... you have loved them even as you have loved me.' (Jn 17:23) If we continue to do this, our new way of seeing ourselves will replace our former depressing vision and we will experience the joy which always follows faith. In brief then, we have to:

1) Notice the telltale sign of some negative feeling
2) Understand what illusion or wrong way of seeing things is causing this feeling,
3) Choose a form of words that express the right way of seeing things and assert them each time we experience the negative feeling.

The essential work of Jesus in the gospel is helping us to 'repent and believe the gospel.' In the following scene we have an example of the way he sought to bring about this change of mind and heart.

On that day, when evening had come, he said to them, 'Let us go across to the other side.' And leaving the crowd behind, they took him with them in the boat, just as he was. Other boats were with him. A great windstorm arose, and the waves beat into the boat, so that the boat was already being swamped. But he was in the stern, asleep on the cushion; and they woke him up and said to him, 'Teacher, do you not care that we are perishing?' He woke up and rebuked the wind, and said to the sea, 'Peace! Be still!' Then the wind ceased, and there was a dead calm. He said to them, 'Why are you afraid? Have you still no faith?' And they were filled with great awe and said to one another, 'Who then is this, that even the wind and the sea obey him?' (Mk 4:35-41)

THE EXERCISE

1) An example of the first level of illusion that we looked at above is the way in which getting angry can easily depress us. It can make us feel that our day was a mess. The truth is that what our anger led us to say or do tarnished only slightly an otherwise very good day. What we replace this distorted vision with may be expressed in words like, 'A lot of good things happened today, so take a bow.'

Take an example of a situation which often bothers you. Describe the kinds of negative feelings it normally gives rise to and the distorted vision which causes these feelings. What words would you use to express the vision with which you hope to replace the distorted one?

2) An example of the second level of illusion we are prone to is the way we identify with recurring feelings of false guilt. Much of the time we give to prayer may be distracted. As a result, we may think of ourselves as failures, where prayer is concerned. The truth of the matter is that being distracted at prayer has got to be seen as part of being human and something we have little control over. So the correct way of seeing ourselves as distracted prayers could be expressed in some way like, 'It's okay to be human!'

Take a situation which seems to belittle you or make you feel inadequate. Describe what happens, how the situation is conducive to a negative self image, and the kind of strong negative feeling this leads to. In what way does the image or vision of yourself become distorted in this situation? What way would you express to yourself, in an apt phrase, the right way of seeing yourself in this situation? Name other situations where you tend to accept the witch's illusion that you are inadequate or not up to much.

3) An example of the third level of illusion is the way that a distorted image of ourselves can resist or block the true image of ourselves. This true image is that which people who know and love us would have us accept or believe. We may catch a glimpse of this illusion in our reaction to someone who pays us a compliment or expresses his or her love for us.

Describe a situation where someone affirmed you or expressed his or her love for you in a way which embarrassed you. Describe how you felt and the way you evaded the affirmation or the love.

Are you inclined to store away the memories of people's love for you and come back and savour these memories often? Is it this third level of illusion which prevents you thus returning to your rich store of memories of people who have loved you?

After quietening yourself for a while, ponder the fact which Jesus wants you to accept in the two passages of Scripture below. After pondering each of them, notice your reaction.

As the Father has loved me, so I have loved you; abide in my love. (Jn 15:9)

I have said these things to you so that my joy may be in you, and that your joy may be complete. (Jn 15:11)

PART III

Introduction to Exercises 11-17

In Exercises 1-3 we looked at our story. In it we noticed patterns that manifest God working out the dream he has built into each of us. In Exercise 4 we saw the importance of coming to know two essential aspects of ourselves, one poor and the other rich. Then in Exercises 5-10 we examined a way of facing our human poverty that can make it a constructive and even a joyful experience.

The next seven exercises are all about the love that is the essential element of the rich, or gifted and graced, aspect of ourselves.

Exercise 11 aims at helping us to explore and own our rich *experience* of the fact that we are loved and loving. We will see how this receiving of love involves ourselves, the persons of the Trinity and the significant people in our life.

In Exercise 12 we single out the love of significant people. These, in the different ways they have loved us, have given us some impression of who God is. They have thus been a source of life and sustenance.

In Exercise 13 we move to the way that God reveals his love to us. We take, as our model for this, the way that God spoke with Moses 'face to face as a person speaks to a friend'. (Ex 33:11) In this dialogue, which prayer is, God discloses himself to us as love, if we choose to listen. Through the second part of the dialogue, that of responding honestly to what we have heard, we may hope to overcome the resistance in us to his love.

In Exercise 14 we accept Jesus's invitation to come to know him as God's love revealed in human terms.

In Exercise 15 we look at the way the Spirit leads us to an intimate knowledge of the love he has 'poured into our hearts'. (Rom 5:5) We also look at how the Spirit is the source of the joy or consolation that follows our acceptance of this love.

Exercise 16 aims at helping us to become more sensitive and responsive to the way the Spirit leads us to appreciate his essential gift of love.

Finally, in Exercise 17, we look at how we respond to the Trinity's revelation of their love for us by loving them and others in return. We will focus more on all that God has taught us about loving, than on how deficient we are at it.

Four loves

I grew up with the belief that faith was what made a person a Christian. It was, however, a faith understood as an acceptance of a body of truths, moral teachings and the practice of certain devotions. It has taken me a long time to discover and appreciate the fact that it is the reality of our being wholly and deeply loved that is central to faith. As we saw in the story about Care on page 11, it is this love which makes and sustains us. As this story is the central symbol we will use in this exercise, it is important to go back and ponder it before moving on.

Care, in the story, is a symbol of the Good News of God's love and the power of this love to enliven us. That we would believe in this love and have our lives transformed by it, is the essential call of Jesus.

> The kingdom of God has come. You must change your hearts and minds and believe in the good news. (Mk 1:15)

It is in order that we would have an intimate experience of God's love and providence that we receive the Spirit's gift of love. The experience of this love is the core of the dream we have to realise.

> Already we have some experience of the love of God flooding through our hearts by the Holy Spirit given to us. (Rom 5:5)

Love as the essential gift

It is the purpose of the Spirit's Seven Gifts to help us explore and own the 'length and breadth, the height and depth' of this love, which would otherwise be beyond our grasp.

> For this reason, I bow my knees before the Father, from whom every family in heaven and on earth is named, that according to the riches of his glory he may grant you to be strengthened with might through his Spirit in the inner man, and that Christ may dwell in your hearts through faith; that you, being rooted

and grounded in love, may have power to comprehend with all the saints what is the breadth and length, the height and depth, and to know the love of Christ which surpasses knowledge, that you may be filled with all the fullness of God. (Eph 3:14-19)

Due to the Spirit's gift of love, we each have a rich store of experience of being loved and of being loving. This experience, however, may lie well below the surface of our lives. It lies dormant, as we have probably never seen the importance of discovering and exploring it. What we may be much more aware of, and trust more readily, is the kind of analysis that leads to an intellectual understanding of our faith. As we saw in Chapter 2, we seem to have neglected being loved and loving 'with our whole heart, soul and strength' for the sake of loving God with our 'whole mind'.

Ways we resist this love

Our contact with the feeling of being loved, and of being loving, is limited as we resist letting it surface. I remember attending a workshop where we were asked to go back to a time in our life when we felt loved. After trying it, people voiced the reluctance they felt at being involved in this kind of exercise and the difficulty they had in identifying an experience to work with. It was, however, also evident from what people reported back that those who had managed to touch this kind of love in their past, were deeply moved by it.

One reason why we may resist making God's love for us central is that we are brought up to believe in the principle of correction. This principle states that we improve or grow through bettering what is below standard about our behaviour. The constant application of this principle generates in us an image of being a disappointment to God, to others and to ourselves. The poor self-image which results from this attitude blocks or diminishes our experience of being lovable and loving.

We may also tend to focus much more on how loving we *should* be and hardly at all on how loving we *are*. We may thus find it difficult to be with all the affirmation that will come out of this exercise. It may seem unreal. This sense of unreality is confirmed by a world in which man's inhumanity to man is so tangible. To make being loved and being loving a high priority in this atmosphere may seem sentimental and irrelevant.

Arousing what is central to our dream

In reality, love is what God discloses himself to *be*, in that God is not just loving but *is* love through and through. The experience of this love is what God most wishes to share with us. Because this love is so central to our life it refuses to lie dormant for long. It keeps surging up into consciousness, as for example when we go to a film that moves us deeply. There is nothing closer to our core than love, and nothing with such power to make us feel alive and happy. The Spirit who has planted this love in our hearts will always be at work helping us to explore and make our own of it.

> I write this to you about those who would deceive you; but the anointing which you received from him abides in you, and you have no need that any one should teach you about anything. You know that the Spirit teaches you about all things, always telling you the truth and never a lie. So as he has taught you, live continually in him. (1 Jn 2:26-27)

It is not analysis, however, or thinking deeply about it, that releases the power of the love which the Spirit wants us to experience. We have to discover, explore and own its creative and sustaining power with our 'whole heart, soul and strength' as well as with our 'whole mind'. So, as well as the meaning of our experience of love, we will have to delve into the images, the feelings, the desires, the symbols and the memories we associate with it. If we do not expose ourselves to this full range of our experience of love, it will remain in an abstract, spiritual world and will not become our greatest resource for life and happiness.

As a way of bringing to the surface a wealth of experience of love which the Spirit has inspired in us, we will focus on four aspects of it. These are the four loves of the title of this exercise. They are:

1) The love God has for you.

2) The love you have for God.

3) The love people have for you.

4) The love you have for others.

THE EXERCISE

1) Start with your experience of the love of God for you. Record some of the peak times in the story of your relationship with God, times when the kind God is for you became clearer. How have

you been led to see God over the years? What would you include in your picture of the kind of person God is for you now? Does this picture of God differ much from the one you picked up from your parents? Note what images of God appeal to you most. What pieces of scripture do you enjoy going back to, as expressing images of God which you warm to?

Note your main positive feelings towards God, when you focus on images of him which you like. Are there images of God that you resist and that make it difficult for you to be at home with him? What kind of negative feelings do these images cause? Is there a symbol or a mantra that would express for you the way you now see and feel about God?

You might like to spend some time in your inner room, noticing, around the walls of it, the pictures, icons and symbols, which express who God is for you now. Dwell with what you feel is the most important picture of God for you and note what it says to you about him.

2) In this part of the exercise you try to form a picture of the way you love God.

Do you think of yourself as a person who shows a lot of love towards God? Are you good at this or just mediocre?

List some times in your life when you expressed your love for God in the decisions you made or in things you did for him. After selecting one of the most important of these times, re-live it by going through what happened step by step. Are there ways that you show your love for God in an indirect way? For example do you show you love by your efforts to be a just or good person, or in the bulk of the decisions you take or the things you do?

What are the main ways that you have failed to love God? Take one example, and after dwelling with what happened and how you felt about this, ask God how he feels about it now. Is he as forgiving and accepting of your failure as the best of your friends might be? Take the picture Jesus paints of God as the father of the prodigal son in Lk 15, and see is God as accepting and as forgiving of you as Jesus says he is in this parable.

Does God appreciate your efforts to love and serve him? Write down the things God would appreciate most about you, and then let him say these things to you. Is God as good at showing appreciation of you as the person in your life who is most conscious of your goodness and also is good at expressing this?

Is God pleased with your overall desire to love him and the way you have tried to give expression to this desire in your life? Spend time trying to let God say how much he appreciates your efforts to show your love for him. Let him express his gratitude to you for this. You may find that you are excessively conscious of your failure to love God and that you need to keep facing the fact that this is an illusion. You will be helped to face this illusion by letting God be at least as appreciative of your efforts to be good and loving, as the best of your friends would be. Also, you may need to dwell with the reality that God delights in you, as he says he does in Isaiah 62:4-5.

3) Spend time with the ways you have been loved by some of the people in your life. Even though we will do this more fully in the next exercise, it is good to get an overview of it in the context of this exercise,

Begin by listing some of the people from whom you have experienced most love. As you look at these people, how does the memory of their love for you make you feel?

Go through an experience of a time in your life when you felt very loved by one of these people. How did this affect you at the time and how do you feel as you renew your memory of what happened? Talk to this person who has loved you and then listen to what he or she wants to say to you now, and what you want to say in reply. Do you find that you resist the love they show you? Do you want to filter down its intensity, until you are comfortable with it?

Do you think that you live most of the time with the illusion that you are not much loved by a large number of people, and that therefore you are not very lovable? What ways do you feel that you are missing something which could enliven you by your failure to accept the love of those who are close to you? Would you like to change this?

4) This part of the exercise is to help you to become more aware of, and enlivened by, your experience of the ways you show your love for the people in your life. There is a rich vein of gold in your

story, created by your fundamental commitment to people. Spend time exploring this by noting down experiences of ways you have shown your love for those around you.

Write down the ways you have been good to the people around you. How do you feel as you do this? Does it give you the desire and the energy to be more concerned for others? Does the good you do outweigh the bad, and which are you more conscious of?

Do you think that God would want you to face the reality of the caring quality of most of what goes on during your day? What would God want to say to you about the positive attitude you have to most people? Let God say this and then tell him how you feel about what he has said.

Note down some of the ways you find that you fail others. Then take one example and after staying with your experience of it, try to accept and forgive yourself for this. Look at it in the light of all the good that you do for others, in order to see it in perspective.

As a way of arousing the experience of your love for others, go back to a particular incident when you showed your love for someone. What did this mean for you at the time? What does it mean for you now? Choose one person you have loved, and spend time with the story of your relationship. Then re-live an incident where you put yourself out for this person. God will be anxious to help you to accept his appreciation of what you did. So, stay with this and see how much of God's admiration and gratitude you can accept. Share honestly with God how good this makes you feel, but also the resistances it gives rise to.

Significant people

God needs to become incarnate to communicate intimately with us. Our relationship with God needs the flesh and blood quality of the way we relate with friends. Without this down-to-earth quality the spiritual can be very abstract so that it is hard for us to feel really involved in it. We therefore need to draw on our concrete experience of friends and the way they touch our lives, to give us some impression of what God'a love is like.

Show them who I am

A young peasant lad was summoned by a great king to come and see him. When he arrived at the palace, the king said to him, 'My kingdom is so large that I cannot meet all my people and touch their lives as I would want to. My wish is that you would give them an impression of who I am.'

As symbols of the new role he was to play, the king gave the youth a sceptre, a robe and a crown. Now, since he did not know the king, the poor lad was very confused about what he was being sent to do. He was too awe-struck to ask the king what he meant, so he went to consult a wise man. He was told by him to go back to his farm and just to be himself.

As time went on, more and more people came to visit him for they found in him a sympathetic ear and a compassionate heart. He gradually realised that this was what the great king had sent him to do. This was the way he was sent to give people an impression of what the Great King was like.

People who open our heart

'Significant people' is a term we will use in this exercise for those people who, by their acceptance and affirmation, have enlivened us. They have given us an impression of God and what his love is like. They are such people as family or friends and they are significant in the sense that by their love they have had much to do with making and sustaining us.

In his book, *Four Loves*, C S Lewis gives the example of the way our friendship with one person is enriched by that which we have with another. So if A is a friend of B, she comes to her friendship with C, with something more to offer, because of what she has been given by B.

In the variety of ways in which significant people love us, they speak to different areas of our heart and open us up to different kinds of love. If we keep these experiences alive, other people can, from then on, speak to these areas of our heart. As a result, we know, in a felt way, what the different facets of love are like. If we do not keep in touch with the heartfelt experience of those who have loved us, the love of God will tend to remain more in the head than a reality that touches our whole heart and soul, mind and strength.

People do not believe in rheumatism or falling in love
until after the first attack. (Mark Twain)

Even if we have fallen in love, but are not willing to return to and relish the power of 'this first attack', we will only have a superficial appreciation of a book like the Song of Songs.

Experiencing God's love in human terms

So the experience of the love of significant people in our lives is the best avenue, and perhaps the only one, to intimacy with God. If this intimacy with God is to become an experience of being wholly and deeply touched by another, we have to experience it at the human level first. It is only then that it can become real and relevant in our relationship with God.

Just as Jesus puts the Father's love in human terms, so we in our turn can give others some impression of what the love of Jesus is like. In this way, we are a sacrament of Jesus's love, just as he is a sacrament of the love of the Father. We continue the work of the incarnation by giving each other an impression of the Great King, of what the love of God is like in concrete, human terms.

We each have a rich store of experience of being loved by significant people. Most of this, however, lies dormant. If it is to be of much use to us, it must be aroused. This will take a determined effort, as it probably lies well below the surface. Arousing it will most likely be resisted as it may seem unreal in the atmosphere of a very unloving world. Yet, it is vital that we arouse the memory of the love of the significant people in our life and be nourished by this essential food of the spirit.

Kinds of significant people

I would like now to look at the four loves that C S Lewis examines in his book *Four Loves*. The four loves are: *affection, falling in love, friendship* and *charity*. These may help to draw out for us the length and breadth, the height and depth of Christ's incarnation of God's love. They will give us a feeling for what this love is like.

1) *Affection* is the love we experience within a family which makes and sustains us in our early formative years. It surrounds us as infants when we experience it largely through touch. It is a deep and enduring love and the memory of it can mean that our parents live on in us for the rest of our lives. It is often taken for granted because it is so much part of our early years. It is probably only when we become parents ourselves that we realise the extent and depth of this kind of love and its power to make and sustain us.

It will be true of all these four loves that we can easily get imprisoned in the 10% or so of them which has been defective. We have to try and free ourselves from this prejudice by becoming aware of the 90% which is positive.

2) Romantice love comes like a whirlwind, sweeping us off our feet. It can, if we allow it, touch us wholly and deeply. Because of this, it can, while it lasts, do more than anything to arouse our deep dream and to get our whole self involved in it. *Falling in love*, or romantic love, according to Robert Johnson in his book, *The Psychology of Romantic Love*, is 'the single greatest energy system in the Western Psyche. In our culture it has supplanted religion as the arena in which men and women seek meaning, transcendence, wholeness and ecstasy.' It comes like a whirlwind, sweeping us off our feet.

I never cease to marvel at the way it can suddenly transform people and make them new men and women. For the transformation to last we need the help of other loves, for falling in love is the most impermanent of loves. It needs the love of friendship if it is to remain faithful in realising all that it initially promises us.

3) *Friendship* is based on sharing, and the depth of the friendship will depend a lot on the level at which we share. Ultimately it becomes the sharing, not just of what we have but the sharing of ourselves especially. It is thus the gift of self in self-disclosure.

Jesus bases the friendship he calls us into with him, on his own revelation of himself, when he says, 'I have called you friends, because I have told you everything I have heard from my Father.' (Jn 15:15) Friendship is the most enduring of loves. It shares not only the other's joy but also his or her sorrow. Being so enduring, friendship can bring to romantic love a fidelity to the end, to death.

4) Charity is the love of God which Jesus puts in human terms for us and which the Spirit 'pours into our hearts.' (Rom 5:5) It is the *love* between Jesus and the Father which we are now invited to share in; 'God has made us welcome in the everlasting love he bears towards the Beloved.' (Eph 1:7)

Charity is best understood in terms of the three loves, affection, romantic love and friendship. The Word of God and tradition draw on these loves to give us some idea of the extent and depth of this love which God has for us. For example, Thomas Aquinas, when he wants to explore what grace or God's love means, uses the symbol of friendship. Similarly St John of the Cross uses the Song of Songs as a symbol of the way in which each of us is God's beloved.

The aim of this exercise is to go on a journey into the memory of those who have believed in us. These are the people who have been a sacrament of God for us, giving us a vital glimpse of what his love is like. It is a long exercise, and thus one from which we should pick and choose what is helpful to where we now are on our journey.

THE EXERCISE

1) List some people whose love has meant a lot to you. A few may have expressed how they felt about you in words, but others will have said it in the concern they expressed through what they have done for you. Try to name what is distinct about the love of each of the persons you have listed. The effort to express this in a word or phrase will help clarify what is distinctive about each of their loves, how diverse are the impressions they have given you of the Great King.

2) Recall some incidents where you felt loved, and then select one to re-live. Re-living is a matter of going through all that was said and done in a particular incident. Let yourself dwell with some significant detail, like words that moved you or a gesture that meant a lot to you. When you have finished, note down what you stayed with, and how re-living it has made you feel. Does it make the whole experience present again, and the love expressed life-giving?

3) Paint a portrait, in words, of one of the significant people in your life. Note what qualities stand out, and give examples of times when some of these qualities became apparent. What images and feelings do you associate with this person? From time to time, read back through what you have written and notice how this affects you. Do you feel the subject of your portrait is a rich memory that was, and is, still life-giving for you?

4) Is there a way that the person in your portrait helps highlight some aspect of love, and thus of the God who is love? Re-read the story about the Great King and describe the way the person in your portrait gives you an impression of what God's love is like. Are there words or images in Scripture that express the impression this person gives you of God? Note what way the person you have in mind helps fill out the meaning of those words from Scripture. Does God become more real for you because of this connection?

Take one of the qualities of the love of the person in your portrait above. See whether Jesus is like this in some gospel scene. As you move back and forth between this person and Jesus, see if it gives you a greater appreciation of this kind of love, in both Jesus and the person in your portrait.

5) In this section of the exercise you are asked to become aware of the ways you resist or reject the love of the significant people in your life.

What way do you react when someone shows they love or care for you? Describe a time when this happened and then say how this made you feel. What, for example, do you say when someone comments on how well you have done some job, or on how good a person you are? Do you dwell with what they say to savour it? Are you more likely to pass over quickly what they say, without taking it in and owning it? When people compliment you, do you, as John Powell suggests you should, ask them to say it again, write it down and put it in your top drawer for further perusal? Are you more likely to partially deny what they say or cut it down to a size you can easily handle?

Working with the principle that God is at least as good as the best person you know, see if you are comfortable attributing to God something you like about the person in your portrait above. Can you let God say to you something as complimentary as was said to you by the person above? How does this make you feel? You may have to ask yourself the question, 'If God is not at least as good as this person, or as positive about me, is he the true God, or a false one?'

6) Sketch, in words and phrases, a picture of a member of your family. Note what effect doing this has on the way you see and feel about this person. Is his or her love different from that of another member of your family? Is there something special to be appreciated about the way they each relate to you?

In C S Lewis's *Four Loves*, he distinguishes the love of affection from that of falling in love, and friendship from charity. As a way of heightening your awareness of a rich store of experience you have of each of these loves, see do you notice much difference between them. Is there a difference between the love you experience from a friend you have and that which you associate with a member of your family?

7) Be with someone from whom you have experienced affection, friendship, or with whom you have been in love. Sketch briefly the story of your relationship, just mentioning the main events in the way the relationship developed. Next say how you see and

feel about that person now, and then enter into a dialogue or conversation about the way you both have seen the relationship and how you feel about it. Write this down as you go along. Start off by saying how you think things are between you, and then let the other person reply. Continue listening and responding honestly until you both have said all you want to say. Finish off by being quiet for a while before writing down how you feel about this experience.

Speaking to God face to face as with a friend

God wants to reveal himself to us, if we are willing to listen. This for me is the most astounding reality there is. Astounding too is our tendency, illustrated in the following story, to prevent this happening, by 'binding up God's tongue'.

God's One Word

God created all with his Word, 'Let it be'. Of one part of this creation however the devil was particularly jealous; he deeply resented human beings and their intimacy with God. He, therefore, bound up God's tongue and mocked God for no longer being able to speak, or to be intimate, with human beings.

After many eons, God pleaded to say just one word to his people, and this the devil conceded, thinking that God could not make up his losses with a single word. So God spoke the one word 'Jesus' to the people he had made, and it brought them great joy. In this word God expressed all that he is, his caring, forgiving and loving self. In Jesus, God was able to say all that had been stored up during his long enforced silence.

When I first came across this story it puzzled and intrigued me. It seemed so improbable that the devil could silence God. As I stayed with it, however, an interesting truth emerged. It is really our unwillingness to listen to God which binds up his tongue. This unwillingness to be receptive to God's Word, means in effect, that God is prevented from revealing himself to us. The story confronts us with the following realities:

- God delights in conversing with us
- sharing not only all that he has, but all that he is.
- This, however, is conditional on our being willing to
- listen and respond to God's self-disclosure.

---

1) Listening

When God seeks to reveal himself through a passage of Scripture, for example, we may find it hard to listen. We would probably feel more at home thinking about it, or working out its implications. So when we listen to a piece of God's word we need to keep an eye out for what strikes us. This will generally be a word or phrase that states some fact about God. We need to let our minds and hearts adjust to this fact, rather than just think about it.

A way of doing this is to repeat the word or phrase, mantra-like, to let what it says about God sink in. By staying with what God opens up for us in this way, we will be able to let it sink down from our heads into our hearts. We can thus make sure it influences, not just how we see God, but also the way we feel about him. We will thus be answering Jesus' call to repentance – to change our minds and hearts, in order to believe what God is revealing to us of himself.

Do we listen to God or to ourselves?
Instead of listening to God's revelation of himself, we can easily gravitate towards thinking about ourselves and what we should or should not be doing. It is important to ask ourselves what we end up with when we are praying with the Word, to see whether it is Good News or 'good advice'. If every time we approach someone we get advice, we will not feel comfortable in their presence. A constant stream of correction drains our energy and enthusiasm.

For example, when we hear God saying to us in, Jeremiah 31:3, that he is constant in his affection for us, how do we react? We can easily turn our attention to how fragile our own affection is or how undeserving we are of this kind of love. It is easy to move from a sense of how far we fall below standard to thinking about how we might improve. This focus on ourselves and how we might do better, is obviously not the primary interest of Jesus. He expresses a deep conviction, that is at the heart of the New Covenant, when he tells us that the primary concern is that we would come to know God.

> I have made your name known to them and will continue to make it known, that the love you have for me may be in their hearts, and that I also may be there. (Jn 17:26)

Does God Speak *to me*?

We will probably notice how we prefer God's love to be said, as it is in the prophets, to the people of God, rather than to each of us personally.

In the Bible story there is a growth in the way people see God. This reflects the stages each person must pass through in coming to know God 'face to face as a friend'. (Ex 33:11])

1) We may see God as a rewarder and a punisher, giving us advice and warning us of the consequences of not following it.

2) God may also be seen as one who loves his people, but relates with each person as part of a crowd. Relating with us face to face is contrary to how transcendant he is.

3) From the announcement of the New Covenant in Jeremiah, it is clear that God wants to make himself known 'to the least no less than to the greatest'. (Jr 31:34) Each of us is now in the position Moses was in when God spoke to him 'face to face as a person does with a friend.' (Ex 33:11.)

We have to move towards letting the full intensity of God's love be said to each of us personally, as this is clearly God's wish. To help bring this about, we might use the device of inserting our own name into every piece of Scripture we pray with. However we manage it, we must let God speak to us face to face as, as to a friend.

Tasting a little

If we really want to make our own of what God reveals to us when we are listening in prayer, we have to be willing to linger with it. Repeating a little in order to let it sink in, will have to become a feature of the way we pray. The quest for novelty and the fear of being bored may make it difficult for us to remain in the one place for long.

God will open up areas of light, attraction and desire and it is important that we dwell with these, giving him a chance to expand and deepen them. So if some aspect of a piece of Scripture is opened up for you, stay there and mine it. There is great wisdom in the following insight about prayer:

> It is not a multiplicity of ideas that will satisfy the spirit
> but to taste a little interiorly. (St Ignatius Loyola)

FOLLOW YOUR DREAM

2) Responding Honestly

If we give ourselves time to take in anyone's love, it is going to stir a lot of strong feeling in us. Try to remember something loving that was said or done to you, and then notice the feelings that this memory arouses. You will probably have difficulty doing this, as you may not be used to becoming aware of, or dwelling with, the feelings it will arouse. You may have been given the impression that 'feelings don't count', and so they lie dormant, not noticed, named or shared. This impoverishes any relationship, but especially that which the dialogue of prayer seeks to build up.

Positive and negative feelings
When someone says, 'I love you' or 'I think you are doing a marvellous job', we have two reactions. We will find very positive feelings saying something like, 'I love to hear you say that, so keep it coming.' There is also a voice that resists what is said, or rejects it as unreal, as too good to be true. In prayer we therefore have to,

- notice how we react, when we listen to God revealing his love,
- put words on our postive as well as our negative reactions,
- share these with God.

In our effort to share our feelings with God, it is not necessary to say them in any but the simplest of ways. When we have strong feelings we want to express to someone, we often rehearse carefully how we will express them: we may not get another chance. We feel the need to word it well and maybe in a variety of ways. What we say to God should have none of this complexity. It would benefit most from being said over and over again in the simplest of mantra-like ways. So, while it is important to notice our feelings and to put words on them in order to share with God how we really feel, the simpler and the more often we say then to him the better.

Our positive reactions
We may tend to take evasive action when strong love or appreciation comes our way. We ought to welcome it. John Powell says somewhere that we should react to praise with words like, 'Would you like to say that again?' There is, however, something in our upbringing that makes this a very strange thing to say, whereas in fact it expresses a very healthy reaction. We need all the affirmation we can get to sustain us on the way.

Sharing our positive reactions to the love which God reveals for us is an essential part of praying. Through it, we intensify the experience of what God says and deepen our experience of very healthy feelings. Through noticing, naming and sharing positive feelings we also deepen them, worship God and share ourselves with him.

Our negative reactions

A large part of us will resist God's strong love and appreciation for a variety of reasons. These include the belief that we don't feel we have earned such love, and that in this world we don't get what we have not earned. Thus God's love may appear unreal and not relevant in a harsh or hostile world. We may also feel that, when we approach God, he will demand changes in our lives so we may feel anxious or fearful.

If we are not to be dominated by these feelings, we have to express them. By doing this, we gain a certain freedom from our relationship being ruled by them. However, in order to express or share these, we have first to notice and name them.

If we don't seek freedom from being dominated by our negative feelings, what resists God's love will remain in place and cause unbelief. This will reduce, like filters, the light of God's life-giving love. It is an essential part of prayer to notice the feelings in us that resist God's love and then to put words on them in order to share them with God

The following quotation may help to highlight how fundamental both listening and responding honestly are to prayer, and to the quality of our relationship with God. The quotation is also an expression of the aim of this exercise.

> The director's contribution to these conversations can be summed up in two key questions: 'Do you listen to the Lord when you pray?' and 'Are you telling him how listening to him makes you feel?' Everything he says about feelings and their articulation is intended to highlight or elucidate one or other of these questions. The first question turns the person's attention to the reality or unreality of the Lord's part in the dialogue. The second addresses the reality or unreality of his own part.
> (*The Practice of Spiritual Direction* , Barry & Connolly)

THE EXERCISE

Open your Bible at Psalm 139 or any other passage of your choosing. Prepare for this exercise by quietening yourself and focusing your attention on something like your breathing. When you feel relaxed, shift your attention to the fact that you are in the presence of God who wishes to reveal himself to you. Next, move down through the following steps:

Step 1: Read the passage of Scripture you have chosen until a word or phrase strikes you, and then pause.

(This is a prayerful reading of the Word, more than a search for its meaning and message. Leave yourself open, therefore, to any word, phrase and image that may express some simple fact about God.)

Step 2:Dwell with the word or words that have attracted you, saying them repeatedly, as a way of listening to them. Next, put in your own name and let God say the words to you personally.

Step 3: Become aware how what God has said to you in Step 2, makes you feel. Notice your positive reactions as well as the resistance you experience. Share these feelings with God as honestly as you can.

(Noticing and naming your feelings in this way may be difficult, but it is an important part of sharing yourself with God in the friendship he wants with you.)

Stay with any sentiment you notice, repeating it in a simple way. Stay with one reaction rather than looking for a variety.

Step 4: Now and again, especially if you have repeated a passage, you may feel moved by what God says to you. If so, rest with this, tasting and savouring it interiorly. However, you should wait to be invited to this step.

(The sign of this invitation is that God opens up for you an area of enlightenment or attraction and you feel drawn to stay with this in order to assimilate it. Keep in mind the principle we had in the introduction, that it is not a multiplicity of ideas which will satisfy you but that you taste a little interiorly.)

EXERCISE 14

What about you?
Who do you say that I am?

Jesus asked this question half way through each of the gospels, when his disciples already had a chance to come to know him. By then they had taken up a stance towards him and they were being asked to reflect on this, and to say where they stood.

This is a question we are always being asked, and even though it may have lost its edge for us, it is still a loaded one. It might be rephrased as, 'Who am I for you?', 'How do you see me?' or 'How do you feel about me?' It is a loaded question in the sense that it challenges us to reflect on what Jesus means for us at present, on whether our relationship is on the move, is becalmed, or stagnant. The question also calls up the whole story of our relationship with Jesus, how it has developed, where exactly it is just now, where it is going, and where we want it to go.

In this exercise we will look at various answers we give to Jesus' question. We will be seeking to find out where we are in our relationship with Jesus, and the way we would like that relationship to be. We will start off with a story which might speak to some aspects of our relationship with Christ.

The miracle of love
Just after the second world war, there was a young girl called Karen who was sent to a transit camp in Palestine. Like Karen, most of the people had been through the concentration camps in Germany, but each person had been differently affected by this experience. It had challenged Karen's desire to help those around her in any way she could, and so she began to teach young people like herself to read and write.

One day she came across a boy of her own age, called Dov, living by himself. Nobody belonging to him had survived, and he had been so badly affected by the experience of the camps that he refused to communicate with anyone. He sat in his little tent all day, apparently just staring at the wall. At least that is what the few people who had tried to advise him saw, and so they had stopped trying to reach him.

Not so Karen. She persisted in coming to see him every day, in spite of his silence and apathy. She was very ingenious in her efforts to get some response from him. Eventually he began to talk, and to show her his drawings which captured memories that imprisoned him in horror.

Through Karen, Dov began to come out of his tent and to talk with others. Then one day tragedy struck – Karen was killed in an accident outside the camp. People rallied around Dov for fear he would again shut himself off but they were amazed to hear him say that things had changed for him as a result of his coming to know Karen. He said that he now wanted to live in a way that would be worthy of her, and of which she would be proud.

What is striking about this story is the way Dov is brought back to life through the down-to-earth experience of Karen's love. This is in contrast with the way in which others tried to help him, by perhaps offering him advice.

What we want to do in this exercise is to come to know Jesus as the Good News, as someone like Karen. This is in contrast with the Jesus who brings us a message with a lot of demanding implications for our lives. This distorted image of Jesus, as one who is always setting us standards and making demands on us, may have been strong in our past and may even still linger. We need to approach him as the one in whom the love of God is revealed to us.

> I am certain of this, that nothing ... can come between us and the love of God made known to us in Christ Jesus our Lord. (Rom 8:39)

Love in human guise

Jesus does not just proclaim the Good News of God's love but continues, in his own person, the Father's revelation of himself as love. So when Jesus says to the first disciples, 'Come and See', he is inviting them, and us, to come to know him as a revelation of the Father's love. Jesus *is this love in human terms.*

Long ago God spoke to our ancestors in many and various ways by the prophets, but in these last days he has spoken to us by a Son ... He is the reflection of God's glory and the exact imprint of God's very being. (Heb 1:1-3)

The dimension which Jesus adds to the love of God is that he makes it incarnate, or puts its full extent and depth in down-to-earth, human terms. What is most distinctive about each gospel scene is that it reveals different characteristics of this love in very ordinary ways.

We may have difficulty meeting him in this way, if we have grown up with an image of Jesus which left little room for his humanness. Our tendency may have been to emphasise the divine side of Jesus to the exclusion, or near exclusion, of the human. In other words, the Jesus we live with may have only a veneer of humanity. This view of him tends to bypass the Incarnation, or not take it seriously enough. In this exercise we will work towards a better balance between the divine and the human in Jesus by emphasising his humanity.

We may find that we resist this change of emphasis. This may be because we can relate, in a less demanding way, with people we keep at a distance, or put on a pedestal. Yet, even though we may have become accustomed to it, this one-up-one-down way of relating with Jesus is contrary to his invitation to see him as a friend, as one who invites us into his own intimate relationship with the Father.

I will not call you servants any longer, for a servant does not share his master's confidence. No, I call you friends now, because I have told you everything I have heard from the Father. (Jn 15:15)

Contemplating Jesus

The over-emphasis of the divine side of Jesus has led to an abstract knowledge of him which lacks flesh and blood. The people who wrote the gospels, however, want us to meet someone they knew intimately. They want to share their personal experience of someone they came to know by being with him day in day out. The writers of the gospels are saying to us in effect, 'We met this person and we were very taken by him; we would love you to have the same experience as we had.' In this exercise we will be trying to accept this invitation, and share their personal experience.

In order to get involved with Jesus as a friend, we will use our experience of the significant people in our life. This experience will help to make the qualities we find in Jesus more colourful and real. We will use the criterion that Jesus must be allowed to be at least as humanly loving as the best people we know.

Another feature of this exercise is that we will approach each meeting with Jesus as a contemplation and not as a meditation. A good example of contemplation is the way that parishioners encounter their new parish priest when he appears on the altar on his first Sunday in the parish. They weigh him up in an intuitive way, rather than in an analytic one. In their minds is the question, 'What kind of a person is this?' So they might say to each other after Mass, 'What do you make of him?' The answer they give would be based on a capacity they have to know others in an intuitive way. We all have this natural capacity for contemplation but we may not have learned to use it.

What can prevent our contemplating Jesus in this intuitive way is our tendency to see the gospels as a message Jesus preached, rather than as a portrait of him. Our training in mental prayer may lead us to analyse any passage from the gospel for its meaning and for its implications about the way we should live. The question we must allow ourselves to be asked each time we open the gospels is, 'What about you – who do you say that I am?' (Mk 8:29)

To answer this question we will have to get to know Jesus in the way we get to know anyone in life. We will have to develop a facility to listen and talk to this person whose deepest desire is to reveal himself to us. How we take in this revelation will be the main concern of this exercise. In it, we will be trying to accept Jesus' basic invitation to repent and believe by listening and talking to him.

Contemplating the gospels

Contemplating Jesus in the gospels will, therefore, take the form of a conversation. In this conversation we will listen to Jesus saying to us personally what he is saying to those in the scene we are contemplating. Anywhere we meet Jesus in the Gospels, he expresses the love of the Father in human terms. He does this in a rich variety of ways and in the most ordinary terms. We have to learn to listen to this love being spoken to us in a personal way through each gospel scene.

Having listened to Jesus in this way, we need to respond as honestly as we can, expressing how we feel about what he has revealed to us of his love. In this way we intensify our positive feelings and overcome our resistance to his love. We will, if we take the pains to notice it, become aware of a lot of resistance within us to the love expressed by Jesus. We need to let this resistance surface and find expression if we are to overcome it.

THE EXERCISE

1) Quieten and centre yourself. Then become aware of Jesus being with you as a friend who enjoys your company.

2) Take a gospel passage which portrays for you some striking quality of Jesus. As you read the passage, let this quality or characteristic emerge and give it time to fill out. Remember that the author is primarily interested in your meeting Jesus, and not in focusing your mind on his message and its implications. In other words, do not allow the focus of your attention to be diverted from the aspect of Jesus's love which you are looking at. If you do, you will end up with what is more like Good Advice than Good News.

3) Next, let Jesus focus his attention on you. Try to let him say to you what, in effect, you have noticed him saying to someone in the scene. The secret here is to let Jesus confront you with his love. If this is to be effective, you will have to choose carefully how you will let him express this love. The tendency may be to let him say things that are bland or too general, that have no edge to them. These will not challenge you with his love.

You might find what St Teresa of Avila suggests helpful, when she invites you to be in his presence and see him look on you lovingly and humbly – or whatever quality you wish to substitute for 'humbly'.

4) If you allow yourself to be confronted by anyone's strong love for you, it is going to stir up a lot of positive and negative feeling. To try this out for yourself, recall a situation where someone said something very loving or complimentary to you. Notice the way you relished what they said as well as the subtle way you resisted it.

At this stage of the prayer, it is vital to become aware of your reaction to Jesus's love and to give it honest expression. More specifically, you have to notice, find a way to express, and then share your positive as well as your negative reactions to the way Jesus says his love for you. There is part of us that hungers for his love, but another that cannot take it in. It is so contrary to the run of our experience, where we are often dealing with the limitations of human love. It is easy in the light of this experience to feel that Jesus' love is unreal.

5) To make his love more real and relevant, you have to see it in the light of your own positive experience of human love. To recall your experience of this from Exercises 11 and 12 you may find the following suggestion helpful. Make a list, down the left hand margin of a page, of the qualities of the love of the people you most admire. Underline the qualities that mean most to you, putting them in the order of their importance. Next, from among these qualities, tick off the ones you think Jesus has, as he is portrayed in the gospel story. If you can, indicate a place in the gospels where you find each of these qualities in Jesus.

6) This part of the Exercise is a way of broadening and deepening parts 2) and 3). In it you select one of the qualities you have taken in 5) above. If possible, *re-live* an experience of it. Then shift back and forth between the way you notice the quality in Jesus and in this person who exemplifies it in the experience you have re-lived. This should add more colour and definition to the way it appears in Jesus. It should also help you to get more involved in the way Jesus expresses this kind of love for you, as was described in 3).

7) The final part of this exercise is a fantasy. Begin this by quietening yourself and then enter your inner room. Spend time becoming attuned with the atmosphere of this most intimate place. Then become aware of Jesus being with you there. Together you notice the pictures and symbols around the walls that represent key times in the story of your relationship. Dwell with some of these images, listening and talking to Jesus about them. Move from the past to the way your present relationship is represented.

When you have finished the fantasy, evaluate what happened in it in the following way. Be sure not to read how you go about this evaluation before doing the fantasy, as it may prejudice the way you do it.

Notice the way Jesus related with you during the fantasy. Was he in general very affirming or mildly affirming? Was he accepting and tolerant of your mistakes? Was he non-committal in his attitude or was he slightly critical? Did he offer you any advice?

Finish the exercise by spending time contemplating the way Jesus dealt with the woman at the well in chapter 4 of St John's gospel. In the light of his acceptance of her weakness and the way he brings to life her strengths, ask Jesus whether he wants to be as accepting and as affirming of you.

Knowing the Holy Spirit

We live in two worlds:

One of these is the outer world of our superficial dream where we spend the bulk of our time. This is a very competitive world where we struggle to make something of ourselves.

The other is the inner world of our deep dream where we are made and sustained by the love of God and the significant people in our lives.

Because we devote so little time and energy to the inner world of our deep dream it tends to appear unreal and even abnormal compared to the practical reality of our outer world. This is the theme of a film called *The Fisher King*.

> The film is the story of four people, two men and two women. Parry, one of the men, is mad, at least by this world's standards. He is obsessed by the Holy Grail which he believes is in the possession of a millionaire who lives in a castle-like residence. Parry's second obsession is Lydia, who appears odd in the way she dresses and acts, but she is the centre of Parry's day. He follows her to work each morning and is in ecstasy when he catches sight of her.
>
> Joe, the second man, runs a radio programme where people phone in looking for advice. The advice he gives them is not very sensitive or concerned, as his main interest seems to be in scoring points at their expense. Very early in the story, Joe realises that Parry's madness is the result of one of his episodes of point scoring. So, driven by guilt, he enters Parry's mad world and gradually grows in understanding of, and in concern for, the realisation of Parry's dream.
>
> By the end of the film it seems that Joe has helped Parry to find the Holy Grail. This is not so much by presenting him with the

cup which for Parry represented the Holy Grail, but by Joe's concern expressed in the trouble he took to get it for him. But it is not just Parry who has found the Grail. Each of the other three main characters in the story also seem to have found it in the give and take of their love for each other. It is as if they are bound together in a fellowship of concern where they each find a new and a happier life in the very human love they have for each other.

What is central for me in this story is the concern which builds up between the four main characters. It is a concern they all receive, as well as share, in the build-up of their relationship with each other. The experience of this down to earth concern influences them profoundly and transforms their lives. I use the word *concern* here, instead of *love*, as it seems to fit the quiet human way in which the characters are drawn together. It is this concern which is the Holy Spirit's essential gift and the object of each person's grail quest.

The Spirit's essential gift

All the versions of the legend of the Holy Grail, like the one in *The Fisher King*, focus on a journey we are all invited to undertake. It is a journey in search of what Jesus calls the 'one thing necessary'.

Martha, Martha, you are anxious and troubled about many things; one thing alone is necessary. Mary has chosen the good portion, which shall not be taken away from her. (Lk 10:41)

What prevents us giving the one thing necessary the time and energy it deserves, is our preoccupation with our outer world, the world of our superficial dream. It might be worthwhile at this point to read again the story about the dream merchant in Chapter 1.

The danger of this tendency to give priority to our superficial dream is illustrated for us in the parable of the Sower. In the parable the weeds, which represent the superficial dream's preoccupation with 'the cares, riches and pleasures of life', grow up around the word and smother it. The whole parable in Lk 8:4-15 is worth reading but here are the key verses:

And as for what fell among thorns, they are those who hear but as they go on their way they are choked by the cares and riches and pleasures of life, and their fruit does not mature. And as for that in the good soil, they are those who, hearing the word hold it fast in an honest and good heart, and bring forth fruit with patience. (Lk 8:14-15)

If we allow our deep dream to be smothered, it gets pushed below the surface of life and becomes dormant. We tend as a result to get confined to a small-minded world of petty interests. It is as if we choose to live in the basement of a beautiful house while God invites us to live in the entire house and to enjoy it to the full. This basement symbolises a world made small by our lack of contact with our true self, with God, with others and with creation. We get cut off from the relationships which are essential to the realisation of our deep dream.

Even though the word of God is smothered and our deep dream becomes dormant the 'still small voice' of the Spirit will not cease its efforts to awaken our dream.

He said, 'Go out and stand on the mountain before the Lord, for the Lord is about to pass by.' Now there was a great wind, so strong that it was splitting mountains and breaking rocks in pieces before the Lord, but the Lord was not in the wind; and after the wind an earthquake, but the Lord was not in the earthquake; and after the earthquake a fire, but the Lord was not in the fire; and after the fire a sound of sheer silence. When Elijah heard it, he wrapped his face in his mantle and went out and stood at the entrance of the cave. Then there came a voice to him that said, 'What are you doing here, Elijah?' (1 Kgs 19:11-13)

This 'sound of sheer silence' or the 'still small voice' is an experience of the essential gift of the love of the Spirit flooding through our hearts.

Already we have some experience of the love of God flooding through our hearts by the Holy Spirit given to us. (Rom 5:5)

We have a vast amount of experience of this love taught us by the Spirit. Much of it, however, lies dormant. There are two possible reasons for our lack of advertence to this great treasure of experience of the Spirit's love. The first is that we may not give the time and attention which we should to the relationships in which we can experience the Spirit's gift of love. Relationships are not a priority in the consumer society we live in today. The second reason is that we may not recognise the love of the Spirit in the incarnate and ordinary way it comes to us. It is in the fund of very concrete concern, like that which the four people in *The Fisher King* experienced from each other, that we must find the love of the Spirit.

Christ dwells in ten thousand places
Lovely in eyes and lovely in limbs not his
To the Father through the features of men's faces
(G M Hopkins)

He will teach you everything
The whole movement of the Trinity's love for us is towards its becoming embodied in our lives. The Father initiates this by revealing his love for us. Jesus puts this love in human terms by becoming incarnate. It is the work of the Spirit to complete what Jesus has begun by guiding us into the full extent and depth of the love of the Father. Through the Spirit, we are led to experience in an intimate and felt way the 'length and breadth, the height and depth, and to know the love of Christ'. (Eph 3:18)

The Spirit is the one who will 'guide us into all the truth'. The word 'truth' as it is used here means the love the Father reveals to us in Jesus.

I still have many things to say to you, but you cannot bear them now. When the Spirit of truth comes, he will guide you into all the truth; for he will not speak on his own, but will speak whatever he hears, and he will declare to you the things that are to come. He will glorify me, because he will take what is mine and declare it to you. All that the Father has is mine. For this reason I said that he will take what is mine and declare it to you. (Jn 16:12-15)

Jesus also portrays the Spirit as a teacher. What the Spirit as teacher will be helping us to become aware of, is the fund of experience we have of being loved, especially by the significant people in our lives.

I have said these things to you while I am still with you. But the Advocate, the Holy Spirit, whom the Father will send in my name, will teach you everything, and remind you of all that I have said to you. (Jn 14:25-26)

Peace and joy in the Spirit

Very closely associated with this work of the Spirit leading us into the full extent and depth of his essential gift of love is the happiness we experience as a result of our owning this love. This owning results in a growing conviction of being loved and this is the essential source of our happiness.

The supreme happiness in life is the conviction of being loved. (Victor Hugo)

This belief that the Spirit is the source of a happiness or consolation which will pervade our lives is expressed in one of the most popular prayers to the Spirit.

Come Holy Spirit, fill the hearts of your faithful and enkindle in them the fire of your love. Send forth your Spirit and they shall be created and you shall renew the face of the earth.

O God, who by the light of your Spirit instructs the hearts of your faithful, grant that by the light of the same Holy Spirit that we may be always truly wise and ever rejoice in your consolation, through Christ our Lord. Amen.

This consolation, which is also called peace, happiness and joy in the Bible, is central to what the Spirit is working out in our lives.

For the kingdom of God is not food and drink but righteousness and peace and joy in the Holy Spirit ... Let us pursue what makes for peace and for mutual upbuilding. (Rom 14:17-19)

In this exercise, we will be seeking to heighten our awareness of our relationship with the Spirit, how it is and how we would like it to be. We will focus too on the love with which the spirit fills our hearts and on the joy that results from coming to know this Love.

THE EXERCISE

1) From your experience in the last four exercises, notice and record some of the different kinds of love which were aroused and became real for you. Note how your experience of these loves differ from each other by recalling examples of each. Ponder the reality expressed in Rom 5:5 on page 121. See do you find a connection between this reality and your experience of different kinds of love in your life.

2) Broaden out your experience of one of the kinds of love which you recalled in 1) by re-living and then recording your experience

of it. Dwell quietly with the reality that your experience of the kind of love you have re-lived is inspired by the Spirit in you. It may help if you imagine the Spirit inspiring you in a way in which someone in your life inspires you with his or her love for you.

3) Be quiet and let yourself be engaged by the atmosphere of a place where you enjoy being alone. Then let the Spirit join you. Allow for the possibility of the Spirit being feminine – the Spirit was assumed to be feminine in some traditions of the early Church. Let her ask you who she is for you. You might find it helpful to recall the story of your relationship. Finally, talk together about how you feel about each other.

Record what the Spirit said to you. Re-read what you have written and notice your positive feelings as well as your feelings of resistance to what the Spirit revealed to you.

For the remaining parts of this exercise and for exercise 16, let the Spirit be masculine or feminine, whichever you feel comfortable with or find healthily challenging.

4) Recall and record the main facts about the Spirit which you believe in. For example, what is the role of the Spirit within the Trinity? What is the role of the Spirit in your life? Arrange these facts in some kind of diagram which would express their relative importance for you. The idea is to get a picture of who the Spirit is for you. What images of the Spirit are most expressive for you of who the Spirit is? How do you feel about these images? Do you warm to them, or are they a bit abstract and cold?

5) Recall some happy people you have known who have also been intent on *your* happiness. Re-live an experience you have had of this quality in one of these people. Then, after quietening and centring yourself, dwell with the reality that the Spirit is at least as happy, and at least as intent on your happiness, as this person. After dwelling with this for some time, reflect on the way it influences your image of the Spirit and the way it makes you feel about her role in your life. Share some of these feelings with the Spirit.

6) Record some of the main events in the story of your relationship with the Spirit. For example, say how you saw and how you felt about the Spirit when you first became aware of the Spirit and how you now see and feel about him. Re-live a time when you became aware of the Spirit and then record what you experienced.

What image of the Spirit emerged from the experience?

7) Be in a quiet place where you like to be with a friend and let the atmosphere of the place grow on you. Recall some points in the story of your relationship with the Spirit and then see where that relationship is now. Anticipate your meeting with the Spirit by deciding on what you want to talk about when she comes. When you meet, enter a conversation in which you both listen and respond honestly to each other. Be prepared to let the conversation go where it will. When you eventually part, remain on in your quiet place, recording what you want to remember of your conversation.

Listening to the Spirit's guidance

In Exercise 15 we looked at the role of the Spirit in our lives. We saw that the Spirit leads us into 'the breadth and length and height and depth' of the love which Jesus has expressed in human terms. The focus in this exercise is on the way the Spirit guides us into an ever deeper appreciation of this love which has been poured into our hearts. We will also seek to face our essential responsibility for letting the experience of this love, which we have explored in exercises 11-15, mould our minds and hearts.

> Do not let the world around you squeeze you into its own mould, but let God re-mould your minds from within. (Rom 12:2 P)

Letting our experience of the Spirit's love mould us is the most creative thing we will ever be asked to do. It is our life's main artwork. It is symbolised by the artist who, inspired with a vision, must first let this vision mould his heart and then find expression in the material he chooses to use. We too must be open to the vision which the Spirit inspires in our heart. Then, guided by the Spirit, we must take responsibility for letting this vision find expression in the way we think, feel and live. We will focus on three aspects of how we might go about assuming this responsibility.
1) It is the Spirit alone who can guide us into realising our dream.
2) The way the Spirit guides us, and
3) How we listen and respond to this guidance.

It is the Spirit who guides us
One of the most difficult problems in evaluating the role of the Spirit in the realisation of our dream is to understand what is the Spirit's part and what is ours. Though we are God's work of art (Eph 2:10) and the realisation of our dream is largely his work, God's designs for us will not be fully realised without our co-operation.

Who feeds the baby?
When we were students studying Theology, it was not long before we came up against one of its major problems. It was concerned with trying to understand how much is God's part and how much is ours, in the working out of God's plan. When we put this to a very wise old teacher we were privileged to have at the time, he replied by asking us a question, 'Who feeds the baby?'

The answer took a bit of working out, but what was sure was that both mother and baby were involved. The mother, surely, does most of the work, but the baby must cooperate, if anything is to happen.

Each of us has a lot of difficulty in life with letting anyone but ourselves be in the driving seat. An even greater problem, however, is with the whole reality of our being constantly guided by the Spirit in the concrete circumstances of a very secular world. In this environment, which shapes our minds and hearts more than we like to admit, God is seen to be more absent than present.

That the Spirit could be always with us, as our teacher or guide, is too much to believe in this atmosphere of unbelief. As a result, we see our best efforts as what we are doing for God, rather than what God is doing in us.

The way the Spirit guides us
The second focus of interest in this exercise is the way the Spirit guides us through enlightening our minds and attracting our hearts.

The Spirit, when enlightening us, opens up a circle of light in some area of our daily experience and then extends and deepens this, bit by bit. This can be compared to teaching, where a topic is opened up and then its meaning is gradually unfolded, according as the pupils are ready to take it in.

The Spirit in this way builds up a picture of reality, putting it together like one does a jig-saw puzzle. This picture of reality is what we are led to see through faith. Then, by means of the Spirit's gifts of understanding, wisdom and knowledge, we are given an intimate knowledge of this vision which faith makes available to us. If we co-operate with this enlightenment, the dream which the Spirit inspires in us will gradually unfold.

Realising our dream as life's main artwork
The Spirit, in leading us into the full extent and depth of his love,
wants us to let this vision shape our mind and heart. The way the
Spirit does this is by attracting us, and building up desires in us
for those areas of our dream which we are ready to realise.

When some desire becomes insistent or a priority, it is an important sign that we are being guided to make a decision and to act
on this. If we act on this decision, we will, like the artist, be called
to evaluate the expression we give it. If what we do is a faithful expression of what the Spirit is attracting us to, we will feel a sense
of harmony, contentment or consolation.

So attractions and desires are an indication of the part of our
dream we are being drawn to realise. The Spirit, as a good teacher,
knows that we can learn only bit by bit. He will indicate what bit
we are now ripe to realise, by building up our desire for it. We
will be strengthened by the Spirit's guidance to realise all those
parts of our dream which are involved in bringing it to full flower.
By inspiring us with hope, the Spirit gets us out on the road towards the realisation of all that is yet to be, of our dream. It is the
role of the Spirit's gifts of piety, fortitude and counsel to sustain
us on our journey into the full extent and depth of the Spirit's gift
of love. Discovering, exploring, making our own of this gift involves a life-long journey.

What do you want?
The ideal is that we would let these desires surface and gradually
emerge as priorities. At some stage we will be ready to say to ourselves, 'I really want this now' and be willing to act on this desire.
The alternative is that we make hollow resolutions in answer to
false expectations we have of ourselves or that others may lay on
us. It was this awareness of meeting expectations rather than following the desires inspired by our dream that led Carl Jung to put
the following inscription over the door of his consulting room:
'Abandon *ought*, all you who enter here.'

There is an important difference here between what I desire and
what others expect of me or what I expect of myself. The world
created by expectations, or 'oughts', is often a very limiting one as
it does not release the energy which desire releases. Where expectations confine us to a small world, desires invite us to realise those

areas of our dream we are ripe for. There is a quotation from St Augustine to the effect that, if God gives us a strong desire for something, it is a sign that he wants to give us the object of our desire. This leads to the final issue we need to look at, which is how we might best respond to the Spirit's guidance.

How we respond to this guidance

As a way of responding to the Spirit's guidance, we will return to the three steps of the process called *reflection*. We are already familiar with these in Exercises 2 and 8.

1) We have to *notice* the way the Spirit guides us by enlightening our mind, and attracting us by building up desires in our heart. It is very important to identify that it is the Spirit who is guiding us in this way.

2) We have to *understand* the Spirit's enlightenment and allow what is opened up for us to mould our mind. We can do this by listening to what the Spirit opens up for us.

3) Finally, we have to *respond* to the Spirit's guidance by taking responsibility for the attractions and desires which the Spirit inspires in us. These attractions and desires are, as we have seen, an indication of the part of our dream we are ready to realise.

THE EXERCISE

1) After you have quietened yourself, recall any moving experience you have had in any of the exercises so far. Enter into that experience again and re-live it. When you are finished, notice any ways you were enlightened, saw something new or saw something in a new way. Next, record how you felt as you re-lived the experience, whether you felt attracted to or enthusiastic about something. Speak to the Spirit about how he was involved in this experience.

2) Whereas Exercise 15 focused on your awareness of the Spirit, this one focuses on how the Spirit guides you and on how you respond to this guidance. Recall and record an experience when you were conscious of the Spirit's guidance and note the way you co-operated. On reflection, what image of the Spirit emerges in this experience? Do you experience the Spirit as male or female? What qualities of the Spirit as your guide are most prominent as a

---

result? What images of the Spirit as the one who guides you do you like? Express in a very simple drawing how you see the Spirit's involvement in your life.

3) Are there ideas, images or feelings you associate with the Spirit which make it difficult for you to relate easily with the Spirit? Record some of these and speak to the Spirit about them. Listen to what the Spirit says in reply. Record how this conversation makes you feel. For example, does it reduce what is getting in the way of your relating more intimately with the Spirit?

4) How do you understand the way the Spirit is involved in helping you to realise your deep dream? What does *Who Feeds the Baby* say to you about your role and that of the Spirit in realising your dream? What does the image of the Spirit as the one who inspires your life's main artwork say to you? How do you envisage this work of art and the Spirit's role in inspiring it? For example, is it like a story you write or a piece of sculpture you create?

5) What pieces of Scripture, which you have come across in this and in the previous exercise, appeal to you most? Choose one and see what it is about it that appeals to you. Try to make your own of this piece of Scripture by using the method of prayer you had in Exercise 13.

6) What way would you express, in a sentence or two, the appreciation of the Spirit you have come to as a result of the various parts of this exercise? Now try to express this appreciation in a few lines of a poem, in a mantra or in a symbol.

7) Recall what it is about your relationship with the Spirit which you value most highly. Enter a dialogue with the Spirit, as you would with a wise friend with whom you share a lot of your experience. Let the Spirit speak to you about how you both are involved in the realisation of your dream, and then allow yourself to reply spontaneously.

The art of loving

The focus of our interest in this exercise is on how skilled, rather than how deficient, we are at the art of loving. How at ease we are with this positive approach will depend a lot on the way we see God relating with us. If we see God as helping us to develop this art of loving, by correcting the ways we are deficient at it, we may feel uneasy with this positive approach.

In this exercise we will assume that God is like the master craftsman in the following story. He is helping us weave even our weaknesses into the beautiful tapestry which is the main artwork of our life.

The Master Craftsman

The tapestry maker weaves his artwork on a piece of gauze stretched across the centre of a room. He is on one side of this while on the other are a number of small boys, each with his own colour of thread from which the tapestry is woven. The tapestry maker indicates where he requires the particular colour he wants to be pushed through the gauze, and the little boy with that colour follows his instruction. But from time to time, one of the boys loses concentration and pushes through the wrong colour, or not at the place indicated. It is very difficult to undo this mistake but the master craftsman, being so skilled, can incorporate it into his plan and even make it a feature of the tapestry.

Rather than turning the searchlight on our failure to love him and others, God highlights the beauty of the tapestry he weaves in our lives. Our weakness and waywardness even become a feature of God's grand design. This intent of the Master Craftsman, symbolised by the story above, is in keeping with the belief expressed in the Letter to the Romans.

... everything that happens fits into a pattern for good. God in his foreknowledge, chose them to bear the family likeness of his Son ... and then lifted them to the splendour of life as his own. (Rom 8:28-30)

That God focuses on affirming, rather than on correcting, is the point made in the parable of the weeds amid the wheat.

He put before them another parable: 'The kingdom of heaven may be compared to someone who sowed good seed in his field; but while everybody was asleep, an enemy came and sowed weeds among the wheat, and then went away. So when the plants came up and bore grain, then the weeds appeared as well. And the slaves of the householder came and said to him, 'Master, did you not sow good seed in your field? Where, then, did these weeds come from?' He answered, 'An enemy has done this.' The slaves said to him, 'Then do you want us to go and gather them?' But he replied, 'No; for in gathering the weeds you would uproot the wheat along with them.' (Mt 13:24-29)

Like the lord of the harvest in this parable, God will not be seeking to eradicate the weeds. What he will be doing is getting us to appreciate, like a friend would, how good the tapestry of our loving really looks.

The effectiveness of God's grace

A lot of our lack of appreciation of how skilled we have become at the art of loving, springs from a false image of God. God is often seen as one who corrects, more than as one who affirms. The result is that we find ourselves the object of God's critical eye, more than of his delight. We have our ear more attuned to Good Advice than to Good News, to how good we should be rather than to how good we are.

When we hear the word of God and homilies on it, we are often left with the feeling that we fall short of what is expected of us. We may even have been led to think of this focusing on our failure as virtuous. This preoccupation with our failure to be loving may also have another cause. It may be due to our failure to appreciate how skilfully the Spirit has been leading us to realise the potential of the love with which he has filled our hearts. (Rom 5:5)

So, in this exercise we will take up what we began in Exercise 11, and try to appreciate how powerfully this gift of the Spirit has influenced our style of loving. This will give us more energy to develop this gift to the full, than any amount of correction. There is a bit of Charlie Brown in all of us. When he was told by Linus that he would never make himself a hero by gritting his teeth, he thought to himself, 'Perhaps, if I gritted my teeth a little harder'.

We are gradually led to make our own of the Spirit's gift of love, the immense potential we have been given to be loving. We are being most skilfully guided to love God and others with our whole heart and soul, mind and strength. So, rather than being preoccupied with our failure to do this, we need to focus on the artfulness with which we have been led to do it.

In his book, *The Art of Loving*, Eric Fromm says that, even though the most important art for human beings is that of loving, it is the most neglected. A lot of our difficulty may be that we do not allow ourselves to see how good we are at this art and what a creative influence we exercise through our loving. Neither do we allow ourselves to advert sufficiently to our memories of people whose concern and gracious courtesy has exercised this kind of creative influence on our life.

> Rich memory of our meeting
> Touches my deepest dream,
> That *love* is alive and active
> In our world,
> And so am I
> Because of yours.
> You have made visible for me
> The God made flesh,
> Born of your concern
> And gracious courtesy.

Repressing our loving self
The main reason why we resist the reality of our being loving is probably that we identify with the 10% of ourselves that is unloving. As a result, we do not allow ourselves to acknowledge how good we are at this art of loving. Nor do we allow ourselves time to let God appreciate and be grateful to us for all the love we have shown him and those around us.

This failure to believe in a God who appreciates and is grateful to us for how loving we are, is the third stage of a major illusion in our lives. The first stage begins with our consciousness of some area of our life where we fail in charity. The second stage is that this failure to be loving gets out of perspective in the sense that, even though it is only a small part of the way we relate with others, we make it much bigger. We may even identify with it as the whole picture we see of ourselves. We are, therefore, unable to take in anything God may say to the contrary. When God comes to tell us of how loving he finds us, we hold up before him, as much more real for us, this reality of our own inability to be truly loving. This curtails or blocks God's efforts to affirm us.

Befriending our loving self
It is as if the loving person that is in each of us has been lost sight of, has been buried under a welter of evidence we have collected of how unloving we are. We are out of touch as a result with the very kind person in each of us who has been deeply influenced by the Spirit's gift of love. We badly need to get in touch with, and befriend again, our loving selves and the constructive power of our courtesy.

Of Courtesy, it is much less
Than Courage of Heart or Holiness,
Yet in my walks it seems to me
That the Grace of God is in Courtesy.
(H Belloc)

THE EXERCISE

1) Begin by setting up a relationship with the person in you who is loving. To do this, ask yourself questions like: What is your initial image of this person? How do you feel about your relationship with a part of yourself whose main concern is loving? Record a memory of a time when you did a good turn for someone and you became conscious of how concerned you are for others. What image do you now have of the loving person in you, as a result of what you have done in this exercise so far?

2) Do you find that you have much respect for your loving self? Would you have as high an estimation of this side of yourself as Eric Fromm has when he says that this loving person in you is engaged in the greatest of all the arts? In what way is your ability to

love a most creative and generative gift? Describe a time when you did something loving and you saw the power of this in another's life. Note down what you think Belloc meant when he wrote that 'the Grace of God is in Courtesy'. Spend time in wonder at the creativeness of this gift.

3) While sitting quietly in your inner room, become aware of all that is represented of your story by the pictures around its walls. Then turn your attention to the tapestry of your life at the centre of your inner room. Become aware of, and admire, the marvellous range of colours of which it is woven, the bright as well as the darker shades. Notice how these dark colours act as a foil for the veins of silver and gold that reflect the richness of your story. After you have dwelt with this, let God say how creative your loving self has been in the making of this tapestry.

In order to let God appreciate your love for him, write down some of the ways you have shown this love over the years, and especially some of the ways you try to give it expression now.

4) Is there a side of your loving self that is weak, that you feel ill at ease with, or that embarrasses you at times with its lack of courtesy or social graces? Record an experience when your failure to be loving in certain ways occupied more of your attention than it deserved. Did this experience colour the way you saw yourself as loving? How does the memory of this experience make you feel about yourself?

5) You may need to become free from being dominated by the 10% of your loving self that is weak or sinful, and that tends to colour your image of yourself unduly. With a view to this, notice, name and share your experience of this 10% of you which is your unloving self.

Return to the tapestry fantasy and, after giving yourself time to get involved in it again, ask God why your unkindness is not more obvious in the tapestry of your life. In reply, let God invite you to become aware that 'he works all things together onto good' for you. (Rom 8:28) Let God ask you to forgive yourself for your unkindness to others and to thus grow in self-acceptance.

6) There are features of your loving self that you may need to stay with in order to appreciate your style of loving. These might be the way you have loved as a child, as a parent, and the way you

loved someone with whom you fell in love. You might consider your strengths as a friend or your life-long love of one of the persons of the Trinity.

After reading Lk 10:30-37, describe the way the Good Samaritan manifests the art of loving in his respect, sensitivity, concern and practical sympathy for the wounded traveller . Recall a time when you were the good samaritan and note down the ways you resemble the Good Samaritan in the way you love others.

In some situation, like that of the fantasy above in 3), let God express his appreciation and gratitude to you for all the love you have shown throughout your life. You might also let Jesus, the Spirit and then Mary, express their appreciation of you in the same way. Mt 25:31-40 may be a good context in which to do this part of the exercise.

7) Prepare for a while to let God appreciate, as he would want to, the rich variety of ways you have shown your love for him. You may need to prepare for this by recalling some experiences of the ways you expressed your love. You may also be helped by dwelling with different images you have of yourself in these experiences of loving God. Then, in the presence of the Trinity, let each person in turn list what they appreciate about the ways you have loved them.

8) After re-reading some of your notes from the above sections of this exercise, be in a quiet place with your loving self. Enter a dialogue where you take turns to listen and speak to each other. Record the dialogue in full or in outline.

PART IV

Introduction to Exercises 18-28

Bringing the Good News to all of creation
We are children of a very damaging divorce. This divorce is between the two worlds of body and spirit, in both of which we are deeply rooted. In Exercises 1-17 we have seen how we are children of an inner world in which we seek to realise our dream. We are also children of the much more obvious outer, material world. What we are seeking to do in Part IV is to re-unite these two worlds to which we belong.

People of two worlds
Ronald Goldman, in his work on the religious habits of young people, has done a lot to help us understand this deep divide within our experience. From his research on the attitudes of young people to religion, he found that they live in two worlds, a spiritual, Sunday world and a secular, weekday one. These two worlds are quite separate, like two circles of experience that do not meet at any point. The result of this separation is that the spiritual world has become unreal and irrelevant, while the secular one has lost its meaning and sense of direction.

Adults are as deeply affected as young people by this divorce. If we are to heal it, we will have to work at reconciling our two separated worlds. This reconciliation involves restoring a lost intimacy between our deepest selves and the various areas of the world of our daily experience. It is a reconciliation which Jesus hopes will result from his death.

> And I, when I am lifted up from the earth, will draw all things to myself. (Jn 12:32)

This theme of Jesus drawing all things together again, by attracting them to himself, runs through St John's gospel. It is a restoration of union and harmony which fulfils a God-inspired dream which the Prophets had. This dream was that the Messiah would re-establish the order there was between the different parts of creation at the beginning.

> He did not say this of his own accord, but being high priest that year he prophesied that Jesus should die for the nation, and not for the nation only but to gather into one the children of God who are scattered abroad. (Jn 11:52)

This reconciliation which Jesus seeks to bring about, means *befriending* all these areas of life from which we have become estranged. What is involved in this process of befriending will be worked out in Exercises 18-20 and then applied in Exercises 21-28.

The Exercises
Exercise 18 will be concerned with deepening our awareness of the two worlds within which we live. We will also examine how we can reunite them by befriending those areas of creation from which we have become estranged.

Exercise 19 will be about cultivating a way of finding the deep significance of all things. This will involve renewing our sense of wonder at the mystery of God's presence in the simplest of things.

Exercise 20 will focus on how everything is a gift of God and as such a wayside sacrament of God's love, presence and providence.

Exercise 21 will look at the gift that our body is. We will examine its true role in being intimately involved in the way we relate with ourselves, with God and with others.

Exercise 22 will examine the importance of the sexual self and the way it contributes to the intimacy of our relationships.

Exercise 23 has to do with leisure as essential for keeping in touch with our dream.

Exercise 24 will focus on work as the place where we give concrete expression to our dream.

Exercise 25 will focus on our inner journey in search of our soul. We will look at how developing an awareness of our invisible male or female partner is essential for growth in intimacy with ourselves, with God and with others.

Exercise 26 will examine the gift of the environment as a 'second womb' within which we are formed. We will look at the basically friendly nature of our environment.

Exercise 27 will look at the exploitation of nature and the quest to restore a lost intimacy with it. We will see how nature has the power to provide us with the solitude we need to get in touch with our deepest selves.

Exercise 28 will focus on the gift of technology and on how we may grow in appreciation of its positive aspects.

Befriending the estranged

In this Exercise we will be concerned with how we might bridge the chasm that has opened up between the spiritual and what makes up most of our daily experience. The origin of this chasm is described for us in the story of the Fall in the book of Genesis. There we find a picture of the disastrous consequences which follow when we walk out of the intimacy for which we are made.

'Things Fall Apart'
By walking out of the intimacy which God had established with them, Adam and Eve became estranged from themselves, from each other and from the created world around them. The harmonious relationship which God established in all things when he created them began to disintegrate. In the story of the Fall we see the radical way this separation from God affected human relationships when Cain murdered Abel. This violence then spread throughout society like an epidemic and ended in the destruction symbolised by the story of the Flood.

In the following lines from one of his poems, W B Yeats depicts for us what happens when what holds our lives together loses its influence: 'Things fall apart; the centre cannot hold':

> Turning and turning in the widening gyre
> The falcon cannot hear the falconer;
> Things fall apart; the centre cannot hold;
> Mere anarchy is loosed upon the world,
> The blood-dimmed tide is loosed, and everywhere
> The ceremony of innocence is drowned;
> The best lack all conviction, while the worst
> Are full of passionate intensity. (W. B. Yeats)

The Great Warrior myth symbolises what happens to our relationships with all else, when the essential one we have with God deteriorates.

FOLLOW YOUR DREAM

The Great Warrior myth

We grow up believing that we live in a hostile world, divided between 'them' and 'us'. The need to defend ourselves against 'them' breeds the mentality of the great warrior. This mentality gradually limits the scope of our understanding and concern to 'our own people'; we adopt a cold, impersonal attitude towards all others whom we entitle 'them'.

The extent of our understanding and compassion is further limited by other attitudes generated by this myth. The belief that women, and the feminine in each of us, do not belong to the great warrior class, leads to a lack of respect for the feminine side of life. Qualities such as tenderness and refinement are regarded as unbecoming the more rugged *esprit de corps* of the great warrior.

This myth, therefore, has a very limiting effect on our relationships, restricting severely the degree of sensitivity and compassion that we show to others. It also leads to a poor relationship with creation, as it justifies a ruthless exploitation of the environment for commercial interests. The myth thus limits what we are sensitive to, and feel responsible for, to a small fraction of what this should be.

The effect of the mentality generated by the Great Warrior myth is that we get imprisoned in a very small world. We get cut off from our essential relationship with ourselves, with others and with the created world around us. We thus become impoverished, by being out of touch with the spiritual dimension of much of what we come across each day.

One of the results of this deterioration of our essential relationships is that the spiritual dimension of creation is excluded from the way we see our world. The disastrous way this is affecting us is described in a book called *The Turning Point*. In it the author, Fritjof Capra, who has written extensively on the philosophical implications of modern science, draws a picture of how damaging our present ways of thinking have become. This is exemplified especially by the mentality that requires the massive build-up of arms which we find in the world today.

There is, however, a great note of hope also in Capra's survey of what is happening in a wide range of the sciences. He sees a quiet revolution taking place in which we are beginning to move to a re-discovery of the profound way all things are related. For example, he notes that many scientists have now reached a view of the role of the spiritual that is akin to that of the great mystics of the past.

> In the twentieth century, however, physics has gone through several conceptual revolutions that clearly reveal the limitations of the mechanistic world view and lead to an organic, ecological view of the world which shows great similarities to the views of mystics of all ages and traditions.
> (Capra – *The Turning Point.*)

'The universe is friendly'
Einstein is at the forefront of those scientists who began to see the world in a more spiritual way, to take an 'organic or ecological view of our world'. In this view, the world is seen as a vast network of things, all interrelated. Everything is made up of a huge array of interconnected parts and these belong in turn to a much bigger system. The harmonious functioning of this vast system is built into the universe and operates automatically.

We humans have to get in touch with how we are related to the rest of creation and be obedient to this relationship. We have, due to the influence of the Great Warrior Myth, lost touch with much of this creation. We need, therefore, to re-establish a true relationship with those areas of creation with which we have lost touch. This is essential if we are to answer the call of Christ to bring the Good News to all creation. (Mk 16:15)

Befriending what was estranged
The word the Bible uses for this restoring of a lost intimacy is reconciliation. This means befriending that from which we have become estranged or separated. As this process of befriending will be central to the exercises to follow, I will say something about each of the three essential stages of it.

1) The first stage requires that we develop our capacity to be receptive, or to listen, to creation. This involves accepting the aspects of creation that we are not proud of. It also involves affirming creation, being open to its wonder and inbuilt wisdom, but most of all to the reality that creation is a sacrament of God's love and providence.

2) Besides learning to listen to creation, befriending it requires that we respond honestly to what we hear it saying to us. This response will be both positive and negative. We will, for example, feel good about the beauty and wonder which creation will reveal to us. We may also find the Great Warrior in us resisting an intimate relationship with creation. We will need to notice, name and share this resistance, as well as our positive feelings, as honestly as we can.

3) As a third stage of befriending any part of creation, we will have to get involved in an ongoing dialogue with it. This dialogue will maintain the listening attitude established in 1), and maintain our capacity for responding honestly which we opened up in 2). Our relationship with any part of creation will be as good or as intimate as the quality of this communication.

THE EXERCISE

1) We described in the introduction to this exercise our experience of living in two separate worlds. Write about how you experience the two worlds on either side of this divide. You might like to draw an illustration of these, using two circles, one inside the other. The relative size of each circle might help you to get a sense of the way you view the importance of your two worlds.

2) What is your attitude to the outer or secular world in which you live? Do you see it as more important or more real for you than the inner one? What images, feelings, attractions do you associate with this outer world of your daily experience?

3) Describe your attitude to your inner or spiritual world. How real and important is it for you compared with your outer or secular world? Make a note of any feelings you are aware of with regard to the spiritual side of yourself. For example, do you feel self-conscious when people talk about spiritual things? Note what images you associate with your inner world. Choose a suitable caption to capture a good deal of how you see and feel about this the deepest side of you.

4) Why, do you think, have these two fields of our inner and outer experience drifted so far apart? Which of the illustrations given in the preceding pages help you to articulate how you see this divide? Describe how your life is affected by this division.

5) Describe what way you see yourself healing the rift or bridging

the chasm between these two worlds you live in. What images, such as those of reconciliation or befriending, best express the way you see this chasm being bridged? Perhaps you have done a lot already to bring your inner and outer worlds together. If you have, mention some key events in the story of this, such as a time you were laid up in hospital, that provided the opportunity for you to be free enough to realize that there is a hunger in you for the spiritual.

6) Read Eph 2:11-22 and notice the way that Paul sees the barriers between our two worlds being broken down.

7) After quietening and centring yourself, set out on a journey to meet a wisdom figure. This may be someone whom you believe has reached a healthy view of creation. As you journey, prepare to meet this person by recalling what has come to you in the course of this exercise so far. When you meet your wisdom figure, listen to this person's reactions to your attitude to creation. On your return journey, reflect on any way you are the wiser for your meeting and jot down your main reflections.

An appreciation of gifts

There is a brief quote from St Catherine of Sienna which thrills me every time I come across it. It strikes a note of hope, it opens up a vision not only of the way that things might be but of the way they are meant to be. It is a vision of life in sharp contrast to the one which sees us as 'weeping and wailing in this valley of tears'. She says,

All the way to heaven is heaven.

I associate what she says with a piece of poetry and a story. Both of these tell us of the richness of simple things and of the joy that is readily available to us in the ordinary of everyday. They build on our hope that what St Catherine is saying might be realisable for all of us, and not just for the few who live at her exalted level. First then the piece of poetry:

Earth's crammed with heaven,
And every common bush afire with God.
But only he who sees, takes off his shoes.
The rest sit round it and pluck blackberries.
(Emily Dickenson)

What appeals to me about these lines is the belief they express that joy is not confined to somewhere apart from where we spend most of our day. It can in fact be found in all things, even the most simple. Earth is 'crammed with heaven' if we would but open our eyes.

The Great Land is here
The story addresses our tendency to mistakenly believe that it is not in the here and now or in the simple everyday things that we will find our happiness.

There was once a famous count who lived in a great castle filled with books. He was reputed to be the wisest man in the world. One day when he was out walking he came across a little child playing on the sea shore. This little fellow was trying to fill a hole in the sand with sea water. The count did not think this made sense, for the water kept disappearing into the sand. After talking to the child about it for some time, he began to realise that it did make sense in the world the child lived in, a place called the Great Land.

This stirred the count's curiosity so he asked how he might get to this Great Land. The little boy pointed to the blank page of a book that lay beside him. The count felt very foolish, but he asked the book how he might get to the Great Land. To his surprise he was told to learn to laugh, and when he had mastered this, to learn how to play, to dance, to cry. However, having mastered all of these, he still had not reached the Great Land.

One day, when he had almost given up all hope of getting what he wanted, he saw some children playing and decided to join them. It was then, in sharing their uncomplicated world of play, in learning to enjoy the simplest things of life, that he realised that the Great Land is here.

Imprisoned in a tiny world

There is a great wisdom in learning to find the Great Land in the simple things all around us. Otherwise we get trapped in a small world built around something which, like the Count, we seek compulsively. We get trapped in a narrow view of things, when, for example, we see them as merely functional. We lose touch with the essential mystery, the awesome aspect of our surroundings. This sense of mystery was what Mark Twain felt he lost when he began work on a steamboat on the Mississippi river. Till then the river had always been a place of mystery for him. When it became the place he earned his living, it lost all of that.

If things lose their mystery and we become preoccupied with their usefulness, they tend to distract us from, rather than put us in touch with, the spiritual side of ourselves. When things distract us from our dream, or our Grail quest in this way, they do not enliven us. What we imagine will enliven us will always remain somewhere other than in the ordinary.

The opening to the top

We all have a basic capacity for wonder, a capacity to find in all things 'an opening to the top'. All things open to God who is always there 'before we arrive'. To be on the look-out for and to respect this truth was the advice a wise missionary bishop used to give to his newly arrived priests.

'Our first task on approaching another people, another culture, another religion, is to take off our shoes, for the place we are approaching is holy, else we may find ourselves treading on men's dreams. More serious still, we may forget that God was there before our arrival'

> Then Jacob woke from his sleep and said, 'Surely the Lord is in this place and I did not know it!' And he was afraid, and said, 'How awesome is this place! This is none other than the house of God, and this is the gate of heaven.' (Gn 28:16-17)

This passage reveals the conclusion Jacob was led to through the vision God gave him of a ladder stretching between heaven and earth. In fact, the ladder which symbolises God's desire to communicate with us, is not confined to any one place but is everywhere and in all things.

> The angels keep their ancient places –
> Turn but a stone and start a wing!
> 'Tis ye, 'tis your estranged faces,
> That miss the many-splendoured thing.
>
> But (when so sad thou canst not sadder)
> Cry – and upon thy so sore loss
> Shall shine the traffic of Jacob's ladder
> Pitched betwixt Heaven and Charing Cross.
> (Francis Thompson)

'Take off your shoes'

What is the mystery in all things to which we wish to gain access? It is an element in everything that causes wonder. This is the most basic element in all things, the imprint of its maker. Our sense of wonder grows out of our effort to appreciate the special worth or splendour that each thing has, quite apart from its usefulness to us. What is deepest in all things, therefore, is their power to speak to us of their maker, of God's grandeur.

> I kiss my hand
> To the stars, lovely-asunder

Starlight wafting him out of it; and
Glow, glory in thunder
Kiss my hand to the dappled-with-damson west:
Since tho' he is under the world's splendour and wonder,
His mystery must be instressed, stressed;
For I greet him the days I meet him, and bless when I under-
stand.

(G M Hopkins)

Each part of God's creation must be allowed to have a life of its
own, a dream it seeks to realise. As we saw in the introduction to
Part IV, all creation depends on us to help it become aware of its
worth. We are sent to bring it the Good News that God 'sees that
it is good' and takes delight in it.

And God said, 'Let the earth bring forth living creatures of every
kind: cattle and creeping things and wild animals of the earth
of every kind.' And it was so. God made the wild animals of
the earth of every kind, and the cattle of every kind, and everything that creeps upon the ground of every kind. And God saw
that it was good. (Gn 1:24-25)

Befriending creation
Besides the mystery which resides in all things, there is the mystery of their intimate relationship with us. Everything created is
related to us and is in some sense a companion, a friend. Laurens
van der Post noticed, in the Bushmen he got to know, this natural
capacity they had to relate with everything in a most intimate
way.

This first man lived in an extraordinary intimacy with nature.
There was nowhere that he did not feel he belonged. He had,
from my observation, he has, I will say, none of that dreadful
sense of not belonging, of isolation, of meaninglessness which
so devastates the heart of modern man. Wherever he went he
felt he belonged, and what was more important, wherever he
went he felt he was known.

We have to work hard to retrieve this view of things that sees beyond their practical use. It is a task we must undertake if we are to
discover their mystery and to befriend all those areas of creation
from which we have become estranged.

The framework of this and subsequent Exercises is based on the

FOLLOW YOUR DREAM

three elements of befriending which we looked at in Exercise 18. The focus will be mainly on a way of opening up the first element in which we seek to come to know, to appreciate and to be in wonder at, the great goodness there is in even the simplest things around us.

THE EXERCISE

1) Make a list of simple things or experiences that you enjoy each day. Notice, for example, what a marvellous gift sunlight is. Take one gift and let it reveal some significant events in the story of its relationship with you. There will probably be images, feelings and desires that these events give rise to. Note these down and stay with anything that strikes you as important, to let it become more real for you.

2) Take something simple that is part of your daily experience and get a sense of how valuable it is in your life. Imagine that you have been told that you will soon be without this. Enter a fantasy where you envisage what life would be like without it. When you are finished, note how you feel and what way you now see what you have been dwelling with.

3) Allow yourself time to quieten down and then focus in on the wonderful features of something ordinary in your life which you are inclined to take for granted. Dwell with how extraordinary it is. When a sense of wonder emerges, stay with this and leave it room to expand. Try to put words on your feelings of appreciation and gratitude. Parts of Psalms 8, or some lines of poetry in the introduction to this exercise, may help you to express your sense of wonder.

4) Spend some time with the way you have taken for granted something like fresh air which is vital for you each day. Notice how unaware and unappreciative you have been of it, and even how you may have abused it. Note down how you feel about this and what you would like to do as a result. Is there a need for you to be forgiven for this failure, to be reconciled with the thing that you have neglected or abused?

Is there much of your daily experience that you have become cut off from, as a result of the Great Warrior myth? Remember how this mentality brings about diminishing horizons of understanding and concern. Has your life been impoverished as a result of your getting cut off from this area of your experience?

5) Take some simple experience, such as that of friendship, and spend some time appreciating it. You could do this in stages, beginning by becoming aware of a friend, for example, and some key experiences of the way he or she has been good to you. Savour one experience of this friendship by re-living it and then stay with any feelings, such as enjoyment or delight, that may arise. Finally, give expression to your appreciation of all that it has meant to you, as well as desiring all it could become for you.

6) Now that you have been with some aspects of your daily experience, note what are your main reactions to any parts of it that you have dwelt with above. For example, you might feel grateful or guilty, more appreciative, or you might feel a greater sense of wonder. Like the Count in the story above, give expression to one or more of your feelings in a spontaneous, childlike way. You may find it helpful to put how you feel in a descriptive phrase or mantra and then say this over and over again.

7) Read the quotation from Laurens van der Post again and choose something, like the stars, with which you would like to relate with more intimately. Recall some experiences you have shared. When you have gained a sense of the stars as your companion, you might make a statement about how you relate with them just now. Next, write down what is the main thing you would like to say to the stars and then let them answer. Continue this dialogue until both of you have said all you want to and then just sit together with whatever realisation or strong feeling of intimacy that might emerge from the dialogue.

8) You might find it helpful to develop the symbolic side of any gift you have used in any part of this exercise. What images do you associate with it? Is there an image from scripture that you think of in relation to water, to air, to the stars for example? See can you express your relationship in a drawing, in a line of poetry or in a mantra.

Finding God in all things

What do you think of the statement, that you have only to be loved a moment to be loved a whole life through? Does it sound a bit unreal in the hard-headed world in which we live? Perhaps it would need a number of conditions to be fulfilled before you could accept it. For example, the memory of the 'moment' when you felt loved would need to be re-lived in some way to keep it alive and active. Again, you would need to develop the facility for getting everyday experience to put you in touch with this memory of being loved.

However, none of us is relying on a single memory of being loved. Each one of us has a store of memories of those who believe in us, people who have loved us and cared for us in a variety of ways.

Counting your blessings
An elderly married pair auctioned their house. As they sat for the last night in what had been their home, it seemed very bare. Just before they went to bed, the husband took out a little tin box which he had saved from the auction. In it were memories of their life together, of the ways they had been blessed, the joys they had shared, and even their times of darkness that had turned out to be blessings in disguise.

As he took these memories out of the box and dwelt on each one in turn, he and his wife were no longer conscious of their stark surroundings. They re-lived the richness of their life together and they were grateful to God.

That night he died in his sleep. When he was laid out, she replaced the rosary between his joined hands with his box of memories. It was with these she knew he prayed best. The evening of the funeral she opened her own store of memories.

There she placed all the words of appreciation of her husband she had heard at the funeral. In the years that remained to her, she was sustained on her solitary journey, by the grace-filled memory of their life together.

The box of memories here might symbolise what we have tried to get in touch with in Exercises 11-17. There we saw in practical terms how we have been touched, wholly and deeply, by the significant people in our lives. We felt also the security, contentment and joy that reviving these memories brings. A whole new dimension will be added to our life if we can find a way of getting in touch with our box of memories through the ordinary experiences of each day.

'Take care you don't forget'
Take care that you do not forget the Lord, who brought you out of the land of Egypt, out of the house of slavery. (Deut 6:12)

We are in great need of the nourishment that our box of memories can supply. Therefore, it is important for us to be able to get in touch with these memories through our daily experience. Our inability to do this is probably due to the rift which has occurred between the ordinary things of our daily experience and the spiritual significance of these things. As a result, much of what we come across each day has lost its meaning. It has become unreal and irrelevant in the atmosphere in which we spend most of our time.

Our problem, of being only able to find the spiritual in a place apart, is illustrated by the example of the electric delivery van. For this to function properly, its batteries have to be charged up every so often. When it is being charged it has to be taken off the road and plugged in at a power point. Then it can be taken out on its rounds again. However, all the time it is out on the road the batteries are being run down, so that at the end of the day it will have to be recharged at the power point.

What we need to do – to continue with our illustration – is to develop a car with a solar cell. This gets its energy from sunlight so that it is being charged up all the time while it is on its rounds. What corresponds in us to the solar cell is the built-in capacity we have to pick up energy from much of what we come across each day. The practical question this Exercise attempts to answer is how we develop this capacity to be spiritually energised by the ordinary experience of each day. How do we develop our capacity to find God's love in the most ordinary circumstances and thus be charged up with the energy of which this love is the greatest source?

An illustration of how this might work out in practice, is given in Jack Dominian's book, *Cycles of Affirmation*. There he says that if a girl has loving parents, they live in her for the rest of her life. There is a big body of love which her parents built into her, and all kinds of day to day experience can put her in touch with their love. We are all familiar with the way that people who upset us can trigger off a big body of anger which has built up from the past. In a parallel way, very ordinary acts of concern can trigger off the experience of the love which God has built up in us over the years.

> God's love has been poured into our hearts through the Holy Spirit that has been given to us. (Rom 5:5)

Letting all things nourish us

All creation is a source of nourishment. This is clearly the viewpoint of the book of Genesis.

> God said, 'See, I have given you every plant yielding seed that is upon the face of all the earth, and every tree with seed in its fruit; you shall have them for food. And to every beast of the earth, and to every bird of the air, and to everything that creeps on the earth, everything that has the breath of life, I have given every green plant for food.' And it was so. (Gn 1:29-30)

The main way all things around us can be a source of nourishment is that they put us in touch with God's love, which is our essential human food. Now, we have the potential to get this nourishment from all things. However, it is a potential which is difficult to realise, as realising it involves a big change in the way we see the world around us. There are three stages in this change.

1) We need to heighten our awareness of the fact that all things are gifts. This will involve taking time to count our blessings and not let the absence of what we desire dominate our attention. There is great wisdom in keeping our eye on the doughnut and not on the hole.

Everything that we possess and every complete gift that we

have received comes from above, from the Father of all lights, with whom there is never the slightest variation or shadow of inconsistency. (Jas 1:17)

2) If something is a gift it is thereby a sign. When someone gives us a gift they are saying something that is often more important than the object given. For example, if we get a letter, what means most to us is not so much the information, as the thought that someone took the pains to write. If all created things are gifts, then God is saying something important through them. Discerning and appropriating this deeper meaning that all things want to voice, takes time and effort.

3) Our daily experience can become most nourishing when the signs become sacraments, wayside sacraments. Now a sacrament is a sign with a difference. It is a sign with immense power to put us in touch with the full extent and depth of God's love. The most ordinary thing can thus become a wayside sacrament if we learn to see it as a gift and thus as a sign of God's love. It is in the realisation of this potential of all things, to trigger off the memory of our being loved, that creation can proclaim the Good News to us.

Seeing the things of our daily experience as gifts and thus as signs and even wayside sacraments involves the kind of change that will need a lot of time and effort. All we can hope for in this Exercise is to make a start down the road towards finding the God who is 'lovely in eyes and lovely in limbs not his'.

THE EXERCISE

1) Recall a time when you received a gift from someone who was important for you. Focus on how real the gift was for you as a sign. Does it seem a bit unreal to give it much significance? What is its meaning for you now? How does it make you feel?

2) Dwell for a while with the reality that all is God's gift; 'What have you got that was not given to you?' (1 Cor 4:7) Take one gift and, in the form of a fantasy, dwell with this gift and ask it what it wants to say to you. Then ask God what he wants to say to you through it. Express your response to what God says. After the fantasy, write down what you realised about the gift, how you now see it and how you feel about it.

3) How would you feel about God saying the following things to you through any gift you have so far focused on: 'I thought of you

when I sent you this gift', 'It is because I love you that I have given it to you', 'I want to be present and draw closer to you through it', 'I am always seeking to provide for you in all things. Even in the most adverse circumstances I am always seeking to make all things work for your good'. (Rom 8;28)

4) Try to get a sense of how richly gifted you are by listing some of your natural gifts, like eyesight, and then some spiritual ones, like your faith or God's word. Do the same for some gifts that are unique to your own story, like for example a person who is very significant for you. Note down your feelings as you contemplate all of these gifts. What are they saying to you as signs, or as wayside sacraments?

5) Take any gift and spend some time building up an appreciation of it. Then move on to develop a sense of it being a gift from God to you personally. Next dwell with the reality of this gift being a sign and what this is saying to you about God knowing you intimately and loving you deeply. Then let God say something like, 'I thought of you and wanted you to have this gift' or 'I want this gift to be a sign that I am always on the lookout for your best interests.'

6) Connected with any of the exercises above, you might like to make use of this prayer of St Ignatius.

I will ponder with much affection how much God our Lord has done for me, and how much he has given me of what he has, and finally, how much, as far as he can, the same Lord desires to give himself to me according to his divine plan. (*The Spiritual Exercises*, No 234)

7) Take a gift God has given you, such as a person who has loved you. Dwell with this gift and then note, if seeing this person as God's gift, releases fresh energy in you for your friendship with this person.

8) After giving yourself time to quieten down, ask for the gift of a discerning heart, what Solomon wanted most in life. (1 Kgs 3:9) Recall some of the ways you have been blest in life and then focus your attention on one of these ways. Dwell with how good it was and then on how much God wants you to enjoy the way you were blest. Let this put you in touch with the image of God's love for you that means most to you. Finish off by expressing how this makes you feel.

---

9) Take a gift that you value highly and dwell for a while with what it has meant for you. Enter into the story of its relationship to you and how you feel about it. Enter into a dialogue with this gift, listen to what it wants to say to you and then express your response to this.

EXERCISE 21

Befriending your body

Much of the abusive language we hear today focuses on the human body. This is indicative of the way we see it. The body would seem from this negative view to belong to that part of ourselves that is called the Dark Companion. This is a side of ourselves that we see as less than ideal, or in a negative way, a side of ourselves that embarrasses us and that we may even despise. Each of us is accompanied on life's journey by a dark companion. Accepting this shadowy figure in our depths means the beginning of healing and wholeness.

The Dark Companion
The central character in Victor Hugo's novel, *The Hunchback of Notre Dame*, is a deformed man who is given refuge in a monastery. He is accused of a crime he did not commit and publicly punished and reviled. When a woman from the crowd shows him compassion, he, for the first time finds himself accepted. He then becomes a power for good in her life, saving her and later the sacred place from a destructive mob. The despised figure of the hunchback, once accepted and cared for, becomes a noble figure that we feel proud of before the story ends.

The body as our dark companion
The traditional vision of the body is that it is the baser half of us, the darker companion of the spirit. There is a great need, therefore, to come to a new appreciation of the body, and of the central role it plays in the realisation of our dream. The Bible sees the body as the sacrament of the spirit, through which we communicate with God and others. In order to arrive at this appreciation of the body, we must identify the illusions we have about it and, as a result, the ways we feel badly about it and abuse it.

The origin of the negative image we have of the body is depicted for us in the story of the Fall, in the book of Genesis. There we see that when we separate ourselves from God, our life falls apart. Where there was harmony before the Fall, after it, there developed a hostility between all things. The body was then regarded as an object of shame rather than a part of all that God created as good. In the creation story there is the repetition of the belief that God found all he had made delightful. Adam and Eve shared this delight and we are told that even though they were naked they were not ashamed. 'And the man and his wife were both naked, and were not ashamed.' (Gn 2:25) After the Fall, however, all this changes and we find that they are now ashamed of their bodies.

> Then the eyes of both were opened, and they knew that they were naked; and they sewed fig leaves together and made themselves aprons ... the man and his wife hid themselves from the presence of the Lord among the trees of the garden ... He said, 'I heard the sound of you in the garden, and I was afraid, because I was naked; and I hid myself.' (Gn 3:7-10)

The body drags us down
We are deeply influenced by a view of the body that has a lot to do with Plato's idea of it. He saw the soul as imprisoned in what, in his view, was very base compared to the spirit. This, coupled with the Manachean view that the body is more on the side of evil than good, has left us with a destructive image of this side of ourselves. Our spirituality has been influenced by these views. They have led us to despise what is seen as an enemy of the spirit and as the source of temptations. These negative views have been confirmed by a fixation with the destructive effect of sins that come from the sexual desires of the body.

The result of all of this is that we repress this guilt-laden side of ourselves. Thus our bodies become like the scapegoat in the Bible, sent out into the wilderness burdened with our guilt.

The body as essential for intimacy
The effect of this repression is serious. It can be seen in the way it influences our relationship with ourselves, with God and with others. In his book, *Urgent Longings*, Thomas Tyrrell makes the point that unless we allow our bodies to become involved in the way we relate with others, we will lack intimacy with them. He describes intimacy as being wholly and deeply touched by another. He holds that unless we allow our body to be drawn into the

FOLLOW YOUR DREAM

way we relate with others, we will not become intimate with them. For fear of becoming physically or sexually involved with others, we will keep them at a distance and become what Tyrell terms 'intellectual porcupines'.

We will, as a result of our fear, keep our way of relating distant and cool rather than risk getting involved in an intimate way. Unless we are willing to let the body be involved in the way we relate with others, it will hinder rather than help our intimacy with them. We will not risk the danger of the relationship becoming physical. So we will continue to be out of touch or cut off from a part of ourselves which is essential for all the relationships of our inner world.

If redemption is the restoration of an intimacy with God and others, that we lost at the Fall, then the importance of the body's role in this is vital. Essential to the Incarnation is that God, by taking on a body, would be able to touch us wholly and deeply in a physical as well as in a spiritual sense. It is striking how deeply involved the body is in the whole approach of Jesus to people.

> They brought to him a deaf man who had an impediment in his speech; and they begged him to lay his hand on him. He took him aside in private, away from the crowd, and put his fingers into his ears, and he spat and touched his tongue. Then looking up to heaven, he sighed and said to him, 'Ephphatha,' that is, 'Be opened.' And immediately his ears were opened, his tongue was released, and he spoke plainly. (Mk 7:32-35)

The Temple of the Spirit
Most communication between ourselves, God and others takes place through our body. If we try to bypass the body, or do not allow it to play its proper role, our knowledge of God will become very conceptual. This abstract way of relating will greatly lessen our capacity to be loved and to love with our 'whole heart and soul, mind and strength'. Our knowledge of how personal God is can easily remain conceptual. It can lack the intimate quality there is in our relationship with those whom we allow to touch us wholly and deeply.

The view we find in the New Testament is that our bodies are the temples of the Spirit. This means that our bodies are, like a temple, a communication centre. They are the best place where we can listen to God's self revelation and the best place to respond to it in worship.

> Do you not know that your body is a temple of the Spirit within you, which you have from God? You are not your own; you were bought with a price. So glorify God in your body. (1 Cor 6:19-20)

The need for reconciliation

One of the effects of the Fall, as it is described in the book of Genesis, is that there is a loss of union and harmony within ourselves. This is what Paul describes as a war he experienced going on between the different parts of himself.

> For I delight in the law of God in my inmost self, but I see in my members another law, at war with the law of my mind and making me captive to the law of sin which dwells in my members. (Rom 7:22-23)

We have a deep need for reconciliation. In other words, we have to befriend all those areas of ourselves from which we have become cut off or estranged. The foundation has been laid for this reconciliation in the way Christ has broken down the barriers that have sprung up inside and outside us. Even though Paul, in the following prayer from his letter to the Ephesians, speaks about the barriers between Greek and Jew, what he has to say refers equally to the barriers we have allowed to be erected between ourselves and such areas of creation as our body.

> For he is our peace, who has made us both one, and has broken down the dividing wall of hostility ... that he might create in himself one new person in place of the two, thus making peace, and might reconcile us both to God in one body through the cross, thereby bringing hostility to an end. (Eph 2:14-16)

When St Paul describes what was revealed to him about the way we are being called by God to relate with our body, it is likely that he had in mind the following Greek fable.

Aesop's Fable

The parts of the body were up in arms. They were tired collecting food for the stomach which they felt did very little work and did not earn its keep. So they decided to go on strike. The hands, for example, refused to collect any more food and the teethe refused to chew it. However, they found that they steadily grew weaker and weaker. In the end they were forced to realise, that even though parts of us may appear useless or not to perform a very exalted task, they are nonetheless vital to our well-being. We must grow to respect them as such.

Paul believes that our bodies and all the parts of them that do not seem to perform a very important function, must be respected. We must grow sensitive and responsive to their very special worth.

But God has so composed the body, giving greater honour to the inferior part, that there may be no discord in the body, but that the members may have the same care for one another. If one member suffers, all suffer together; if one member is honoured, all rejoice together. (1 Cor 12:24-26)

So in this exercise we are concerned to build a new relationship with our body. This is what we might call a sympathetic relationship in which we strive to become sensitive and responsive to it as the object of God's delight. In practice we will seek to befriend all those parts of our body from which we have been estranged.

THE EXERCISE

1) Try to get a sense of the identity of your body by listing its parts. Dwell with some of these, noticing the value of the role each plays in your day. Which feature of this most intimate companion do you appreciate most? Which would you find it hardest to do without?

2) Take one of your senses, like eyesight, and note how it is with you as a constant companion. Next focus in on its make up and allow a sense of wonder to grow as you dwell on its complexity and on how efficiently it works. Finally, spend time being grateful for this gift in a spontaneous and simple way. You may find that Psalms 8 and 139 will help you to put words on how you feel.

3) Take one part of your body, such as your hands, and spend time imagining that you have been told that within a short time you will lose them. Go through the details of how you are told this and get in touch with how you would feel and how you would react. What would you want to do before you would lose your hands? Does this help you to appreciate how much this part of your body means to you and how much you may have taken it for granted?

---

4) Write about the way your body helps you to come to know and be intimate with yourself, with God and with others. Become aware and note down the part your faculty of hearing plays in these three relationships.

5) Outline the ways you have related with your sense of touch in your story. Note, as you go along, how you have viewed and felt about touch in the past and then outline your attitude to it now. Conclude with a dialogue with your sense of touch, writing down what you say to each other as you go along. When you have both said all you want to each other, express how you both feel about each other as a result of talking together.

6) What parts of your body are you ill at ease with? Take these, one by one, and notice the image you have formed of each and the feelings which each part arouses. Express to your body what images you have of it and how you feel about it and then let it answer. Listen to this and see what response you want to make. Continue with this dialogue until you both have said all you wish to. Writing down the dialogue, in full or in outline, as you go along.

7) Choose an image that represents the role your body plays in your relationship with God, with yourself, and with others. Be with your body as represented by your image of it. Talk to each other about the way you have related and the way you would wish to relate. At the end, sit together with your body, as your most intimate companion, and express how you feel about each other.

Befriending your sexual self

The sexual in us can be a very creative force but it can also be a very destructive one. Dante, in his relationship with Beatrice, found inspiration, energy and a creative wellspring. Anthony, on the other hand, was besotted by Cleopatra and as a result he lost all his inspiration as a leader.

In one of Woody Allen's films, *Another Woman*, we have the unfolding of the story of a woman's attitude to her passion, her feelings and her sexuality. At the beginning of the story we meet her as a successful lecturer in philosophy. She is very intellectual and controlled. She appears to be devoid of passion and shows little feeling, apart from being embarrassed when her friends talk openly about their sex life. It is when she tries to move further into her intellectual ivory tower, in getting away to write a book that her world of reserve is taken apart.

As she begins her book, she overhears a young woman in an adjoining apartment talking to her therapist. She is drawn into their conversation as she finds it echoes her own experience. We watch her as she re-lives the memories that are aroused in her by what is happening next door. She gradually realises how stifling her feelings, for the sake of intellectual pursuits, has led her to a loss of intimacy and authentic relationships.

Through going back to the memory of someone who had fallen in love with her, she learns to believe again in the possibilities in her own life of feeling and passion. As a result she experiences a sense of peace for the first time in many years, and she finds that the creativity to write her book is released.

Three attitudes to our sexual self

The big question the film asks is, 'How do we see and feel about our sexual self?' There are three answers commonly given by people to this question. Each answer is dictated by an attitude which determines the role we allow our sexual self to play in our life.

Repressing the sexual self
1) The first attitude to our sexual self is illustrated in the film by the very cool attitude of the woman towards her friends. She is embarrassed when they talk about their sex life. She has a very detached attitude to this side of herself and refuses to let it get in the way of her intellectual pursuits.

She typifies a very common attitude which likes to keep the sexual self under tight control. This need may be aroused by fear resulting from a bad experience of getting sexually involved. We are determined that we will not be hurt again. Again the fear may be of our sexuality as a source of temptation and sin. In the past, sins against the sixth and ninth commandments were judged to be the most serious sins and this attitude still leaves a residue of reserve and suspicion about sexual matters.

The effect of seeing our sexual self in a negative way is that we may repress it. Whatever the motivation, this repression of a part of ourselves, which is essential for intimacy, has a damaging effect on our ability to relate with ourselves, with others and especially with God. Then our sexuality, far from being something which we find good, becomes an object of shame, a part of ourselves we want to hide.

> Then the eyes of both were opened, and they knew that they were naked; and they sewed fig leaves together and made loincloths for themselves. (Gen 3:7)

The quest for intensity
2) In the second attitude, our sexual self is identified largely with sex. Here the intensity of the sexual is central and obscures any deeper concerns such as the intimacy which the sexual side of us can facilitate. Then when this sexual intensity wanes or ceases to be, there is little left to hold people together, and so they move on to someone else who can provide the intensity they see as central.

The fruit of this myth, that intensity is the be all and end all of our sexual life, is that we do not enjoy any real intimacy with others. We try to rest our intimacy with them on an emotional level of feeling. We thus refuse to face the fact that real relationships are much more dependent on a conviction of the personal value of the other person than on feelings of emotional intensity. The result of leaving our relationships at an emotional level is that the way we relate remains superficial.

Repression and intensity as a denial of life
Failure to incorporate the sexual into our relationships in either of the ways outlined above has a deadening effect on us. This is the thesis of a book called *Urgent Longings* in which the writer Thomas Tyrell outlines the ways that our relationships with others do not reach maturity without the inclusion in them of our healthy sexual self. Without the sexual, our relationships with ourselves, with God and with others, lack intimacy and do not involve our whole heart and soul, mind and strength, as the Great Commandment says they should.

When the sexual side of ourselves is not properly involved in our relationships, it loses its meaning. It is no longer understood or respected. It is either under-used by being repressed, or it is over-used when its intensity becomes an end in itself. So the immense energy of our sexual self can be used for lesser ends that fall short of the intimacy it has a unique capacity to promote. Thus we can fail to channel this vast source of energy into the creative work it was designed for. The true role our sexual self is meant to play in the realisation of our dream is the subject matter of the third view of our sexuality.

An energy for intimacy

3) This attitude to our sexual self is based on the belief that it is part of a much broader way of relating with others. In this view our sexuality is seen as a gift of creative energy for realising our dream of intimacy. In his book, *Urgent Longings*, Tyrell defines this intimacy as an ability to be wholly and deeply touched by another. Looked at in this way our sexual self can become a powerful help for realising the ideal of the Great Commandment. Our sexuality can become a key element for realising our dream of being loved and loving with our whole heart and soul, with all our mind and strength.

The sexual provides an immense range of energy, from the most earthy to the most mystical. The Song of Songs provides a good example of the richness of the potential of the sexual self. The

Song is so earthy in its eroticism that it is one of the books whose right to be included in the Bible has been most questioned. At the same time it is the book about which most commentaries have been written in the monasteries of Europe. The mystical depths of this book have been explored in the most profound writings of saints like Bernard and John of the Cross.

Our sexuality can be a most creative energy not just for romantic love but for the growth of this love into friendship. In our sexuality we have a unique power to combine the intensity or passion of our being in love with the depth and permanence which friendship can bring to our intimacy with God and with others. It is in providing the energy to undertake the discipline of sharing our innermost selves which friendship requires of us that the sexual side of us can become most creative.

The first two attitudes towards our sexual self are very limiting. The first attitude represses the sexual self and does not allow it to play its proper role. The second makes the sexual side of us too central and asks it to bear a burden which is too much for it. Both attitudes mean that we get out of touch with or estranged from ourselves, from God and from others. There is a need therefore, for *reconciliation*. This means taking the three steps involved in *befriending* our estranged sexual self.

a) We have first of all to acknowledge the innate goodness of our sexual self and the help it is meant to be towards intimacy with others. This will mean, meeting and coming to know our sexual self, allowing time for its value, and for our sense of respect for it, to grow and to be expressed.

b) Befriending our sexual self will also involve responding honestly to the sense of wonder, for example, that arises when we become aware of the creative power of the sexual side of ourselves.

c) A third element in the way we and our sexual selves can befriend each other is through ongoing communication. This will mean that we will have to be ready to listen and respond to basic symbols of this sexual self, triggered off by our daily experiences.

THE EXERCISE

1) Become aware of each of the physical parts of your sexual self. Be with each in turn, noticing its natural goodness and then be

with the wonder of each part in itself. Allow a sense of praise or gratitude to grow and be expressed. At the end say how you feel as a result of doing this.

2) What words would you use to describe the role of your sexual self in the way you relate with men and women? Has it a positive role to play? Do you find yourself wary of the way the sexual may get in the way of how you relate? List some of the ways the sexual side of you influences your relationships in a healthy way.

3) What is the story of your sexual self and the way you have been led to relate with this side of yourself? Are there significant events in the growth of the way you see your sexual self? Are there images and feelings that come to mind as you recall the ways you have related sexually with others? Are there attractions or desires about how you are now being led to let your sexual self relate in a deeper way?

4) Spend some time getting in touch with where your relationship with your sexual self is now, and then begin a dialogue with it. Let each side have its say in the dialogue, and then let each reply to what the other has said. Let the dialogue be guided more by how you both feel than by what you think. Write down the dialogue as you go along.

5) Various people open our heart to different kinds of love and then God can speak or reveal himself to those parts of our heart. Does the way that people relate with your sexual self help or hinder your relationship with God, Jesus, the Spirit and Mary? Do you tend to keep your sexual self apart from your spiritual life?

6) How do you react to the Song of Songs? What words would you use to describe your reactions? Are there some images you associate with the Song which you like, and are there some you feel uneasy with? Is there a way that God can reveal aspects of his love for you through the imagery of the song? What words of the Song are you at home with when God addresses them to you? What words are difficult for you to accept?

7) Are there aspects of the sexual side of you that you are not at home with? Express these as best you can. After spending time in some quiet place let Jesus join you as a friend. Let him ask you to tell him about those areas of your sexual self with which you are ill at ease. Share these with Jesus and see how this makes you feel.

You might then ask him how he feels about you. Let him accept you where you feel weak and let him point out how much he appreciates the way you handle this side of yourself. You might like to confirm how he does this by looking at how he deals with people like the woman in Simon's house in Lk 7:36-50.

8) Jesus says he wants us 'to proclaim Good News to the whole of creation.' What way do you think does Jesus want you to bring Good News to the sexual side of yourself?

Leisure

When I was a student there was a book called, *Leisure The Basis Of Culture*, by Joseph Pieper, doing the rounds. Most of my fellow students read it and were impressed, even though as students leisure had not yet become a real problem for us. I sometimes wonder whether they ever read it now, and if they do, how they react. I have some dog-eared notes on the book which I often return to, as what Pieper says still speaks to a deep need in me.

The theme of the book is that we tend to live with a concept of work as something which demands our all. This concept can easily result in our becoming imprisoned in a very confined area of life, marked out by the expectations that this 'total work' situation makes on us. We no longer have the sky for our limit as we are meant to.

The sky's the limit

There was once a poultry farmer who was given a present of an eagle's egg. He decided to experiment with it, so he put it among some eggs a hen was hatching out. In due course it emerged with the other chicks and grew up with these. Even though it was never quite the same as them, it adapted itself to their ways and always thought of itself, and acted, as one of them. So it spent its time with the other chickens within the strict confines of the barnyard.

One day when it was about a year old its eye was caught by the inspiring sight of an eagle in full flight and something stirred within it. However, its gaze was soon brought back to earth, by a cock telling it to stop star-gazing and to get on with the job.

Now, there are two endings to the story. One has the young eagle putting its head back down as it had been told to do and continuing for the rest of its days within the very limited world of the barnyard. The other ending is, that the young eagle inspired by the vision in the sky, stretched its wings and took off. From then on it was no longer confined to the barnyard but had the sky for its limits.

We also have to choose between living within the strict confines of the barnyard and having the sky for our limit.

Being confined to the barnyard

Without real leisure we cannot have the sky for our limit, but get confined to the barnyard. Work easily becomes so important that all of life must centre on it. This means that we can easily become prisoners in the small corner of life, that this concept of work confines us to. The automatic result of making work our king is that all else must take second place to it. Other areas of life, such as our relationships with family and friends, are pushed into the background; their priority rating being in fact measured by the time we devote to them.

This pushing of important areas of life into the background leads to a severe impoverishment of life. We cease to be enriched by what should be central, i.e. our relationship with ourselves, with God and with others. These relationships have to make do with what is left over after our task-master, work, has taken the lion's share of our time and energy.

'There is no king but God'

There is an African story about a man who refused to allow anyone or anything but God be his king. He used to meet the unjust expectations of others, and even those of his king, with the words, 'There is no king but God!' A lot of pressure was put on him to submit, especially to the king's demands, but he would not budge in his determination to hold God's due place as sacred. After a lot of persecution, he was eventually recognised as admirable, in his devotion to what was right. People were, however, inclined to admire, rather than imitate, his prophetic stance.

This story echoes Jesus' teaching about there being only one thing necessary.

Martha, Martha, you are anxious and troubled about many things; one thing alone is necessary. Mary has chosen the better portion, which shall not be taken away from her. (Lk 10:41-42)

No one can serve two masters; for a slave will either hate the one and love the other, or be devoted to the one and despise the other. You cannot serve God and wealth. (Mt 6:24)

We all, to some degree, become prisoners of our work or something else which we make central. 'Do you not know that if you present yourselves to anyone as obedient slaves, you are slaves of the one whom you obey?' (Rom 6:16) This means that we no longer give due time and attention to what should be our priorities. When we get out of touch with these priorities we are impoverished as human beings and as a result experience restlessness, loneliness and sadness. In this situation where work becomes king, leisure is seen as an escape from the pain of work's frustrations. This means that our leisure activities are not allowed to become serious or to involve much effort; there is a preference for what diverts, or for the trivial.

Where antiquity thought that we should work to have leisure, we are leisurely for the sake of work. Leisure is seen as a means of recovering from work or as preparing for its fresh demands.

Having the sky for our limit
We all know the effect of a good holiday, the way that after it we can again see life in perspective or see it whole. Leisure is meant to be such a time when we can again see life whole. As such, leisure is an effort to be free of the confinement of the barnyard in order to have the sky for our limit. By means of our leisure time, we can pierce the clouds, or the restricting canopy of our own false expectations and those of others. Leisure can become 'an opening to the top' whereby we seek to find perspective and freedom through keeping in touch with our dream.

The Field of Dreams
In a film called *The Field of Dreams*, a farmer walking through his maize field one day, hears a voice from another world. The voice says, 'I will come if you make space for me.' To answer this call the farmer does something which everybody feels is crazy, because they are not in touch with his or their own dream. In obedience to his inspiration, he turns his best field into a baseball park. By doing this he made space to return to a very nourishing memory of the past. This was the memory of

his father and their shared enthusiasm for their heroes in the baseball world. It was as if at leisure times like these he came to know his father as a friend and that he had now to retrieve this memory and sustain himself with it.

Cultivating our field of dreams

Leisure involves setting aside space to cultivate our field of dreams. It means making space to realise our dream. As we saw in the first chapter, this dream is all about the give and take of the basic relationships of life. It means being loved and being loving, as well as the joy that is born of this. This dream is about a heroic journey we are called to undertake, in order to make our own of the full extent and depth of the love of the significant people in our lives.

This may seem very serious business to be entertaining during our leisure hours. It is, however, merely following what is our basic interest or what, deep down, we really want or desire.

Soul, self; come, poor Jackself, I do advise
You, jaded, let be; call off thoughts awhile
Elsewhere; leave comfort root-room; let joy size
At God knows when to God knows what; whose smile
's not wrung, see you; unforeseen times rather – as skies
Betweenpie mountains – lights a lovely mile.
(G M Hopkins)

The Sabbath Day

We tend to think of Sunday or the day of rest as a time to recover from the stresses and strains of work, or as a breathing space to prepare for fresh endeavour. In fact, the idea of the Sabbath in the Bible is more accurately related with the idea of leisure being put forward here. Thus understood, the Sabbath is meant to provide a space for us to have the sky for our limit, to broaden our spiritual horizons. Its main concern must be the realisation of our dream of being intimate with our deeper selves, with God and with others.

Remember the sabbath day and keep it holy. For six days you shall labour and do all your work, but the seventh day is a sabbath for Yahweh your God. You shall do no work that day ... For in six days Yahweh made the heavens and the earth and sea and all that these hold, but on the seventh day he rested; that is why Yahweh has blessed the sabbath day and made it sacred. (Ex 20:8-11)

FOLLOW YOUR DREAM

A time to dream

The following illustration may help draw out the meaning of the Sabbath and the need we have for genuine leisure.

Re-awakening a dream of intimacy

A married pair begin to realise that they are drifting apart. They are, to all appearances, happily married and seem to get on well together. They themselves, however, know that this is superficial, that they are avoiding the deeper issues. They both lead very busy lives, so that they do not spend much time together, and when they do, they keep well away from discussing the reasons for their drifting apart.

Eventually they decide to do something about their situation and they go off on a holiday together. They feel threatened by the prospect of being alone with each other, and of not having the means to escape this. However, they really want to become closer again, and so they spend a lot of time together. Some of the time they share enjoying themselves, but they also make the effort to talk over, in an honest way, what has been going on between them. At times this is painful, but they stay with it.

Before the holiday ends they feel that they have touched again what brought them together in the first place. They are moved by the reality that they are still in love, and by the possibility of this love developing into a deep friendship. They also realise that they will have to make space in the future to continue what they have begun on their holiday. They will have to keep in touch with their deep dream and continue to share it with each other.

The following aspects of this illustration may help us get a clearer idea about the meaning of leisure.

1) Disentangling themselves

There is, first of all, the element of the pair getting away from it all, of standing back from their situation in order to get things into perspective. The holiday provides them with the possibility of detachment from what diverts them from the essentials of their life together.

There is a great fear in us of being separated from our normal source of security. It is very threatening for us to be suddenly deprived of the outer sources of our worth and to learn to rely on our deep inner ones. It is to these inner ones, however, that leisure is meant to provide access. So this first element of leisure is meant to help us attain freedom from what prevents us being in touch with our dream.

2) Making Space

What the pair going off on holiday together require freedom for, is to have space to be with each other. If we are to become intimate with someone, we will have to be willing to spend time alone and with that person. This I think is the meaning of Jesus' invitation to 'come apart to a quiet place and rest a while'. (Mk 6:31)

It is difficult for us to provide the space for this, to find the time and to make the effort it requires. However, it is the condition that the voice in *The Field of Dreams* sets down when it says, 'I will come, if you make the space.'

I spend a lot of my time with people who are anxious to move ahead on their inner journey. I find that for them to make the space they need for this is a vital decision. If they do not make it, there is no chance of them finding what they want.

3) Being face to face as friends

The reason why the pair need to have space is to enable them to communicate with each other. This communication is the essential activity that should take place within the space which leisure seeks to provide. They need to listen and then to respond honestly to each other as the basic necessity of their becoming intimate. Their relationship will be as intimate as their ability to communicate.

4) Rekindling our dream

What the pair would hope to find by making time for a holiday, is to touch again what brought them together, to rekindle the dream they had when they fell in love and got married. The ultimate purpose of leisure is that we would each get in touch with our deep dream and take responsibility for realising it.

THE EXERCISE

1) When you were a child you played, escaping to a world that was more real for you than the one in which adults lived. Do you still allow yourself to play in this sense, and what form does it now take? List some of the ways you play as an adult. What way do you feel, having made this list?

2) What place does leisure have in your average day? Are there different ways you enjoy yourself? Which do you value most? Is leisure more important for you than work, or does it take second place? Are you content with this situation?

3) In your story do you notice much of a role for leisure? Did this role change as your story unfolded? List some of the ways you used to enjoy your leisure, alone or with others. Dialogue, as you have done in previous exercises, with the child in you that needs to play, to have fun and to enjoy simple things.

4) Are there different levels of leisure in your life? What are the deeper ones? Draw a diagram which would convey the relative importance of your leisure activities. Are there images and feelings that you associate with leisure? For example, how do you feel on Friday evening and what image does it call up for you? What is your deep desire for this leisurely side of yourself? Are there things which you can only promise yourself when you retire? How do you feel about retirement?

5) What are the roles of these different kinds of leisure you enjoy? Is there a common purpose to them all? Is leisure, for example, just escaping from the boredom of work? Does your leisure really add a dimension to your life that is equal to or more important than that which work contributes?

6) Would you like your life to have a lot more leisure? What kinds would you like to include if you could have any kind you wanted? What would be the purpose of these? Would they be to make life more tolerable in the barnyard, or would they be to have the sky for your limit? In the kind of fantasy you have done previously, enter into all the circumstances of a visit to your wisdom figure. Listen to what this person says to you about the story *The Sky's the Limit* and what it has to say about leisure in your life.

7) Do you identify more with your work than with your leisure? Would you agree with Aristotle that we are unleisurely in order

to have leisure? Are you leisurely in order to work harder? Would you agree that 'leisure is not a restorative, a pick-me-up for work, but that a person should continue to be a person, to see life and the world as a whole'? (Pieper, *Leisure the Basis of Culture*)

8) Is there a way that some of your leisure activities keep you in touch with your deep dream? Should Sunday have something of this purpose or does it have any distinct role in your week? Does the word Sabbath in the third commandment or Jesus' call to rest, in Mk 6:31, have much significance for you?

Life's main artwork

In Chapter 1 we saw that the dream built into us, like that in the acorn, constantly moves towards maturity. We also saw that our dream can reach this maturity, only if we take responsibility for realising it. It is in this feature that our dream differs significantly from the dream in the acorn. Whereas, in the acorn, the dream is automatically realised, we have to choose:
1) to get in touch with ours, and
2) to take responsibility for giving it expression.
This must be the essential work of our life, our life's main artwork.

We are all called to be creative, to be artists. We normally associate this calling with a small number of specially gifted people. The great cellist, Pablo Casals, had a different view, he had a firm belief in the fact that no matter what work we do, we are all artists. His view counteracts the elitist image we may have of art, and of who are the really creative people. How good we are as artists will depend on our ability to ensure that the job we do helps the much more fundamental work of realising our potential as human beings.

There is treasure in every field
An old man gathered his children around him as he lay dying. He told them that though the farm was small, he was leaving it to all of them, as there was treasure hidden in the land. He said this would support them when he was gone.

After his death the whole family set to work to find the treasure. They dug every inch of the land, even though it took them months. However they found nothing. They were disappointed. but somehow they found a unity and a contentment in working together which they had not known before. To prevent people becoming suspicious of their real motives for all the digging they were doing, they planted the land with crops. They found, to their surprise, that they lived comfortably off the fruit of these.

The following year they dug the whole farm again, but this time they went deeper. Again they found nothing. However, they did not feel that their father had deceived them, because they were coming to realise that the treasure he had promised them, was theirs in working together and in the simple joy of each other's company.

The inner and outer elements of work

Like the members of this family, we often set out to look for what we might call the outer treasure. In the process, however, we discover an inner one like the deeper relationship the members of the family found. It is in finding the proper mix between the inner and outer elements of work that we become creative and allow the artist in each of us to emerge.

> The greatness of an artist lies in the building of an inner world, and in the ability to reconcile this inner world with the outer. (Einstein)

So much of our work today is not creative or joyful because we are out of touch with all but the outer thing which we produce. Our basic creativity will degenerate if we separate the outer aspect of our work from the spiritual vision that is meant to inspire it. The Swedish film maker, Ingmar Bergman, laments the sterility that results from this lack of sensitivity to the inner world that should inspire our work.

> It is my opinion that art lost its basic creative drive the moment it was separated from worship. It severed an umbilical cord and now lives its own sterile life, generating and degenerating itself. (Bergman)

The healthy mix

So work will become degrading when it is separated from the dream that should inspire it. The reverse is also true, in that our dream must be given expression in the earthiness of work, or it will remain unreal. There should, therefore, be a healthy interplay of the inner and outer elements of work. The two should feed each other. It is when they are divorced that both are impoverished. A

FOLLOW YOUR DREAM

colourful expression of a healthy relationship between the two elements of work, is the story in the introduction to Part V, about finding the lion in our hearts before we can find it in the stone. It would be worthwhile to read the story and to see what it says to you before going ahead.

The true creativeness of work

So much of the work we do is dominated by commercial interests. These are like the one with which the family in the opening story, set out to dig the field. It is, however, very important for us, as it was for them, to broaden these interests, if we are to find the deeper kind of treasure as they did.

Our functional view of work today, seeing it mainly as a means of earning our living, makes it difficult for us to find its role in the realisation of our dream. We may be inclined to think that these more elevated views of work don't butter much bread. However, even though the deeper meaning of work may not immediately appeal to us, it is worth staying with, if we are to find the treasure it is meant to be.

What gives work its most profound significance is when its role, in the realisation of the potential of the image of God in us, is fully appreciated. Being made in the image of our Maker, we have been created in the likeness of one who is supremely creative. This power of creativity must centre on the realisation of all the potential of the image of God in us.

In the image of the truly creative One

There are two implications of our being made in God's image which are important for understanding the deeper significance of work.

1) We are, as Paul says, 'God's work of art'. (Eph 2:10) This art-work, that we are, is not yet complete, so we have to get in touch with what has been begun in us by God and take responsibility for bringing his dream in us to full flower. This is the main art-work of life. To realise this we have, like the sculptor, to get in touch with our inbuilt dream or the lion in our heart. We have then to take responsibility for giving our dream expression in the lion in the stone or in the way we shape our lives.

2) Our being made in God's image is immediately associated in

the book of Genesis with our responsibility for the rest of creation. This means that we are called to be partners of God the creator and as such, co-creators. We are made in the likeness of our creator, supremely creative one. This means that we are heirs to God's talent for being creative and are as such invited to continue the work he has begun.

The primacy of concern
If we choose to adopt the above vision of work, what we do during our working day must become subordinate to a much more important spiritual reality. The priority must be given to the way we relate with our inmost self, with God and with others and to the love which is central to these relationships. This love must be the main thrust of our work, for to love is the most creative thing we can do. It is Care, as we saw in the story in Chapter 1, which makes and sustains us. It is in the exercise of this care or concern that our work becomes truly creative and part of our life's main artwork.

This is a very difficult concept of work to live up to today where work is king, and as such demands the bulk of our time, effort and resources. This is a situation that we can do little to change. The little we can do is to set about changing our own vision of work and the attitude we take to it.

Work that creates injustice
There is a view of work that sees it as demanding our all, so that we have little time and energy left for much else. Work in this view is all-consuming. In effect, this means that people who are caught up in this approach to work may have only a minimal amount of time or energy left at the end of the working day for themselves or for others. Their relationships, which should be central, have to take what is left over, and that is often not enough to sustain good relationships.

This is a fundamentally unjust situation where an area of life demands much more of us than it is due. As a result everything else has to take second place and a healthy sense of priorities is lost. The consequences of this are symbolised in the story of Nebuchadnezzar. He sought power so much that he cut himself off from all else and so became dehumanised.

Sovereignty is taken from you, you are to be driven from human society, and live with the wild animals; you will feed on grass like oxen, and seven times will pass over you until you have learnt that the Most High rules over the kingship of men. (Dan 4:28-29)

To make anything central, besides the essential relationships of our life, is to become, like Nebuchadnezzar, dehumanised. 'There is no king but God.'

If what we spend most of our time working at is separated from the dream God has built into us, it becomes, as Ingmar Bergman says, sterile. It gets cut off from what makes it really creative.

Work that creates life's main artwork
Seeing work as centring on life's main artwork or the realisation of our dream, may appear starry-eyed. Yet, a foundation for this concept of work has already been laid. A lot of the positive energy of this century has focused on developing a more caring attitude towards people's working conditions. This care or concern shows in the solidarity there exists among people who work together. Care for those with whom we work is a priority. This foundation needs to be built on, for it is this kind of love, concern, or care, that makes and sustains us. It is what makes our work truly creative and part of life's main artwork.

THE EXERCISE
1) Begin to get a feel for your world of work by writing an outline of your story as a worker. List the places in which you have worked and say what your experience was in each of them. What are some of the maxims you live by when you are at work? Describe or draw an image you have of yourself as a worker.

2) Focusing on the positive side of yourself at work, write about some significant events that were good work experiences for you, and then say what you have learned from these. Describe situations where you feel positively about work and say why they are positive for you.

3) Write about some of the negative experiences you have had of work. Recall situations where work became a burden for you or was boring. Note down the images and feelings you associate with times like these. What negative aspects of work would tend

to dominate your day, or even your whole life at work? Is your working life largely negative or is it positive for the most part?

4) How much of the ideal of work outlined in the introduction to this exercise would you identify with? How much of it would you find yourself at odds with? Note what images you warmed to of those given in the stories and quotations. Write out what you would consider to be a healthy attitude to work that you would like to adopt.

5) How much of what has been said on the more destructive aspects of work do you feel is saying something to you? Write down briefly what you consider are the destructive aspects of work and note your feelings about them. What images of this side of work are most expressive for you?

6) Now, enter a dialogue with work. Prepare for this by recalling what you have already written in 1) about the story of your working life. Then make a brief statement about where you are with work now. As in all these dialogues, imagine work as someone who plays a big part in your life and who wants to establish a better relationship with you. Exchange views on different aspects of your life at work. Let both sides listen and respond honestly on each aspect of work about which you wish to share. Make sure it is not just a sharing of ideas but of your whole selves. Therefore, include some of the feelings and images you have noticed so far.

7) A fantasy about work may help you to bring to the surface aspirations you have in this area of your life. The circumstances of the fantasy are very important, so it is good to spend time on a journey to a wisdom figure whom you wish to talk to about your work. On your way, reflect on one or two of the more important issues you want to talk about with this person. When you have decided this, enjoy the rest of your journey.

When you arrive at the place in the forest or on the mountain where your wisdom figure lives, talk with her or him about what most concerns you in your work. Listen and respond to what she or he has to say. When you are finished talking, write down the lights and the desires you have experienced during your conversation and clarify these with your wisdom figure before you leave.

In search of your soul

So many problems used to be put down to sexual repression, but in our time the main object of repression is our deepest self, our soul. However, this side of ourselves refuses to be silent. It keeps asserting itself and surging up from below the surface of life, demanding that we deal with such an innate need.

How basic it is for people today to meet this need is the point that Carl Jung sought to make in his book, *Modern Man In Search Of His Soul*. Society today is very out of touch with its deepest self, with its soul. As in St Augustine's time, people today, more than ever, seem 'to pass themselves by'.

> Men go abroad to admire the heights and mountains, the mighty waves of the seas, the courses of rivers, the vast extent of the ocean, the circular motion of the stars, and yet pass themselves by.

Yet, judging from films made in recent years – and these must be a fair reflection of what preoccupies us at present – this deepest side of ourselves refuses to lie dormant. Films like *Awakenings*, *The Field of Dreams*, and *Shirley Valentine*, manifest a real search going on within us. They are evidence of our perennial search for our soul and its deepest aspirations. There is a Greek Legend that attempts to explain the extraordinary persistence of this quest and how the male and female side of each of us is involved in it.

The Perennial Search

Plato records a Greek story of how, in the beginning, men and woman were one being. They were joined, back to back, so that they could see in all directions and be in touch with all that was going on in the world around them. With their four legs and four arms they could respond to all eventualities with great skill. This human being who was a rich combination of the powers of man and woman was a perfect creation.

The gods, however, became jealous of so powerful a being, so they split it in half. Ever since men and women feel incomplete by themselves. So they spend their lives trying to get back together again with their other half.

The dangerous imbalance

I have noticed, in helping people on their inner journey, that men and women go about this search in very different ways. Women are much happier than men to be on this journey but are daunted by the prospect of finding a way to go about it. Men, on the other hand, are not as at home with this journey as women are, but they find it easier to plan their journey when they do get down to it.

The different forms which this basic quest has taken over the centuries is described by Martin D'Arcy in his book ,*The Mind and Heart of Love*. In it he describes the struggle that western civilisation has experienced in trying to achieve a balance between these two sides of itself, and the disastrous effects of having an imbalance between them. The same human struggle is experienced in Chinese philosophy. There it is seen as a struggle to keep a balance between the Yin and the Yang, between the male and female in our world and within each person.

If we do not face this imbalance of the male and female within us, it can have disastrous results. This imbalance is most obvious at a cultural level today where there is an almost exclusive stress on masculine values. As a result, we live in a very aggressive and war prone world and this is just one of the many effects of this unhealthy imbalance.

It is difficult to accept that we are each only half a person and thus involved in a life-long quest for our other half. However, coming to know and appreciate our deepest selves faces us with the task of developing a relationship with our other half. For example, the female side of women will be most highly developed and the male side will be weak. This means that if a woman is to mature fully and find her deepest self, her soul, a large part of her effort will have to be concerned with developing her weaker male partner.

Finding your deepest self

We each travel life with our invisible partner, one that lives in our unconscious. So, for example, the male side of a man will be ready to hand in his conscious life, whereas his female half or partner will be invisible, hidden away in his unconscious. He will suffer a terrible impoverishment by remaining unacquainted with his invisible partner. His search for maturity will involve befriending or becoming intimate with this half of himself from whom he is separated or estranged. We have to go to a lot of trouble to meet and come to know this deepest and most hidden part of ourselves.

The name used by Carl Jung for this other person in us is our *animus*, if we are women, and our *anima*, if we are men. These are the feminine and masculine versions of the Latin word for *soul*. Carl Jung worked on the belief that our main task in the second half of life is to get to know and to take responsibility for our invisible partner. For him, this was not an optional extra but an essential concern. If we neglect it, we will suffer the tragic effects of remaining unacquainted with our deepest selves.

Even though our invisible partner may appear insignificant, as not immediately apparent to the eye, Jung compared it to an ocean in which our more obvious male or female side is a small island. This means that there is an immense richness available to us in developing a sympathetic relationship with our unconscious half. On the other hand, if we leave our invisible partner in our unconscious, we become humanly impoverished.

The question then that faces each of us is, 'How do we develop a sympathetic relationship with our invisible partner?'

The two journeys

In her book, *Knowing Woman*, Irene Claremont de Castillejo uses the term 'inner clarity' to describe what the female and male sides of us are searching for. Women have the 'inner' part while men have the 'clarity'. The *animus* or male side of a woman will be seeking a clear way of expressing the inner world with which she is familiar. She will, in the words of this author, be seeking 'to know what she knows and to articulate this'. The man's *anima* or female soul will be putting him in touch with his inner world, which he can then give expression to, with his facility for clarity.

The woman's journey

From my experience of helping people as they journey towards realising their dream, I find that women approach this from a very different angle than men. There are elements of a woman's dream which she is naturally at home with, while others are a

---

problem for her. A woman will welcome the prospect of being in her inner world. She is at home with the relationships, the feelings and the intuitions which form a large part of her inner world.

A woman finds difficulty gaining clarity about where she is on her journey, where she should be moving, and how she should get there. It is with the specifics of this disciplined effort to realise their dream that women find most difficulty.

A woman in search of her soul then, seeks clarity. She strives to 'know what she knows and to say it'. Arriving at this clarity means in practice becoming proficient at the four steps of reflection and prayer. These are symbolised by the four tasks which, in the following legend, Aphrodite assigned Psyche.

Psyche and Eros
When Eros took Psyche as his wife, she was never allowed to see his face. He always came to her by night and departed at dawn. He laid it down as a condition of their marriage that she should never seek to come to know him or ask him questions. When she disobeyed him, and tried to get a glimpse of what he was like, he left her and went back to his mother Aphrodite. When Psyche eventually found him, Aphrodite, who was very jealous of Psyche's beauty, set her four very difficult tasks. She hoped that these tasks would make Psyche go away and leave her son alone.

The four tasks
1) Psyche's first task was to sort out a big bag of all kinds of seeds. This seemed so impossible that she fainted at the prospect, a fact which symbolises how difficult it is for a woman to become aware of and articulate about her inner world. So while a woman finds herself at home when dealing with her relationships, feelings and intuitions she has difficulty putting words on these experiences. A practical example of this task and its difficulty is in Exercise 1. There we tried to sort out the different kinds of experience which made up our story by *noticing and naming* events and the images etc which they aroused.

2) Psyche's second task was to collect wool from a fierce ram. This task symbolises what a woman has to do to understand her inner world, so that her experience becomes focused. So Psyche collects the ram's wool off the bushes rather than directly off the ram. This

symbolises the fact that she must use sufficient of the masculine side of herself to achieve clarity about her experience. She needs to concentrate on forming an overall picture or a synthesis of what life is about for her, a vision that will give her life meaning and direction. In practice this is like what we were trying to do in Exercise 3. There we sought to *understand* the recurring patterns of meaning we found in our experience.

3) Psyche's third task was to collect a small amount of water from the centre of a fast flowing river. Rather than wading into the river to achieve this, she had to find a way of procuring the water without being engulfed by the river. This task symbolises a woman's need to appropriate her experience she has understood, bit by bit. Rather than wading in and being overwhelmed by her experience, she needs to select a little she needs to make her own of just now and to digest a little at a time. She must learn to savour a little interiorly, for it is only this that will satisfy her spirit. If a woman moves around too much in her inner room, and does not allow herself to focus on the little she needs to assimilate, her destructive animus will control her. This destructive animus reveals itself in sweeping opinions that are not based on her own reflection.

In practice the woman's task at this stage is like what we were at in Exercise 2. There we were trying to *discern* what God was drawing our attention to, so that we could make our own of it.

4) With these three tasks accomplished, and with the abilities they develop, a woman must go on her inner journey in search of her soul. This is symbolised by Psyche's fourth task when she was sent off into the underworld. From there she had to bring back some ointment that would make Aphrodite more beautiful. When Psyche got her hands on this ointment and returned to earth with it, she tried to avail of its powers to beautify herself. The effect it had was to put her to sleep. Her search for outer beauty meant that her soul's deep dream became dormant. On her journey in search of her soul, a woman must not allow herself to be sidetracked by anything that would prevent her from becoming sensitive and responsive to her dream.

The man's journey

My experience of men on their inner journey is that they are at home with doing things. They prefer to deal with facts and ideas, rather than with feelings and intuition. They like analysing the meaning of situations and the implications of these for action. They have difficulty letting things move from their heads down into their hearts.

Much of what is involved in God's plan to restore an intimacy that we have lost, would seem foreign to men. They find it easier to be responsive to their own plans, rather than to tune in to those of others. For men, listening or being contemplative is much more difficult than doing. Having to put aside their plans, in order to make space to relate with others or to reflect and pray, does not come easily to men.

As a symbol of a man's essential quest in life it would be worthwhile to read and ponder the Grail legend in Exercises 6 or 15. This inner journey which man must go on means in practice that he needs to devote himself singlemindedly to the love of Christ symbolised by the Grail. A man must make receiving this love, and sharing it, central to his life. He is easily seduced by the intensity of relationships and by the quest for power and control. All this can prevent his taking responsibility for his own inner journey. Instead, he invites a woman to carry his soul for him. To overcome this unhealthy tendency, a man must use his gift of reflection to cultivate the following feminine aspects of himself. These are essential for attaining the love which is the object of his grail quest and for realising his dream of intimacy.

Elements of intimacy
Relationships: A man's projects or work can easily force his relationships, which constitute his inner world, to take second place. He has to learn to be increasingly at home with the intimacy of the relationships which God's love opens up for him.

'Feelings don't count' is the belief of the masculine culture that has formed us. A man must learn to be aware of his feelings, to name, to own and to share them. Thus learning to handle his feelings, a man lays the foundation of intimacy with himself, with God and with others.

The intuitive approach to life, which is second nature to women, needs to be cultivated by men. This is especially true in a world in which rational analysis is seen to be so important. The 'grasp' of God's love, that is made available to us through the seven gifts of the Spirit, is had more through intuition than through rational analysis. (Eph 3:19)

FOLLOW YOUR DREAM

The inner journey is very difficult in a cultural situation where men tend to let their inner world be dominated and diminished by the outer world where work is King. Rather than leaving it to a woman to carry his soul for him, a man must take responsibility for his own Grail quest. It is his responsibility to discover and explore, take possession of and integrate into his life, the love that is the object of his grail quest. It is into 'the length and breadth, the height and depth' of this love that God seeks to guide him.(Eph 3:14-21)

Symbols are the preferred approach to life of the feminine in us. However, our culture's preference for the conceptual has left little room for the symbolic. To be out of touch with the symbolic means that much of the language of the inner world is foreign to us. The three main resources we have for our inner journey: our own story, the Word of God and the sacrament of the Eucharist, are each fundamentally symbolic.

The aim of this exercise is to help each of us, male and female, to become more aware of, and to appreciate, how important is this search for our soul. Motivated by this appreciation we will, it is hoped, set out on our journey towards befriending our estranged invisible partner.

THE EXERCISE

1) Begin by describing any way which you have noticed your invisible partner emerging in your story. What difference did this incident you have described make in your life? There is a history to your relationship with this other half of yourself with whom you seek to become intimate. List some outstanding events in this history? What images do you have of your other half? Do any of these tell you much about the way you see and relate to your invisible partner?

2) Would you like to get to know your invisible partner better? What would be gained from this? How are you, or might you be, enriched by his or her presence? What would you miss out on most if you were deprived of the company of this companion? Is your growing acquaintance with him or her somehow connected with the realisation of your dream?

3) Describe any resistance you feel to coming to know your invisible partner. Do you feel that what is blocking you from relat-

ing is due to some prejudice of yours about men or women? Use the method we had before, of noticing, naming and sharing, to help you discover what is hindering your relationship with each other.

4) Go to some quiet place where you like to be alone or with an intimate friend. Quieten yourself in the atmosphere of that place and then let your invisible partner join you. Talk together about some issue that has emerged from 1) and 2) above. Let both of you say how you feel about it and what way you would want things to be in the future. Write down the dialogue in full or in outline. When you are finished note how you feel about each other and see what symbol you would choose to express your relationship.

5) Are there aspects of the way your invisible partner emerges in your life that you are not proud of? Could you bring one of these before a person of the Trinity or Mary and allow this weak side of you to be accepted?

6) List some ways that your masculine or feminine partner is making himself or herself felt in your life. Describe one of these and then let yourself be encouraged in doing this by one of the persons of the Trinity or by Mary. For example, a man may be learning to appreciate the feminine quality of his own life or that of others, and he may need to have his struggle to do this appreciated. A woman, for example, may be focusing her attention on areas of her inner world so that she might clarify the meaning of her experience, and the direction in which she knows she should move.

7) What way does the destructive non-admission of your invisible partner show itself in your life? For example, as a woman do you notice when your angry man is at work, or as a man do you notice your moody woman?

8) As a woman, what kind is your invisible partner, and how does it differ from a man's? Why is it important for you to search for your soul or your animus? What might happen if you do not? Judging from the tasks which nature invites you to undertake, which of the exercises we have already covered would help you in your search for your soul? One of the following suggestions might help you.

What ways of using the steps of reflection seem practical for you?

Are there ways in which we have approached the exercises so far that might help you develop your animus? For example, do the six steps down the well to your underground stream (Exercise 1) prove useful for you? Write down your comments on the relevance to you of the four tasks assigned to Psyche. Is there much similarity between the first three tasks and the three steps of reflection we had in Exercises 2, 8 or 16?

9) As a man, what kind is your invisible partner and how does this deepest self in you differ from a woman's? Why is it important for you to search for your anima and what might happen to you if you do not? What form does your search for your feminine soul or anima take? For example, do you find yourself making more room in your life for your inner journey? What are you searching for on this journey and why is it an important quest? What practical steps can you take to find the object of your search? What ways do you find yourself getting side-tracked on your journey in search of the Grail? Do you notice much resistance in you to the changes which this Grail Quest calls for? Do not leave the answers to these questions in your head. As you journal about them, include any experiences you find relevant, as well as the intuitions, images, feelings, desires and symbols which these might call up for you.

Our environment

We have mixed feelings about our environment. There are many areas of it that we may feel badly about as well as much that we find sustaining. It is very healthy for us to face the limitations of the surroundings in which we live, as well as to be constantly expanding our appreciation of all the richness we can find there.

Children of our past
The film, *The Prince of Tides*, is the story of Tom Wingo and how he came to terms with the environment in which he grew up. There was much about this environment that he loved and much that he hated. He loved his family, the South and many of the people in the small town where he lived. He hated the endless war that went on between his mother and father and what this did to his brother and sister. Most of all he hated himself because of the memory of an absolutely degrading event that was the source also of his sister's suicidal attempt.

As we enter the story, Tom is trying to deal with the paralysing effects of his self-doubt. To save himself and his sister Savannah, who is in hospital after attempting suicide, Tom is helped to confront his past by a psychiatrist called Susan Lowenstein. Together they unravel all that he hated, as well as all that he loved, about the surroundings in which he grew up.

By the end of the story he had come to terms with most of the circumstances of his past. He had come to accept all the limitations of his environment and to appreciate the fact that the good that was there far outweighed what was bad.

Circles of influence
We might imagine our environment as a series of circles, one outside the other. In the innermost circle we might have the reality that we are the children of two families, that of our father and that of our mother. We have inherited the wisdom as well as the preju-

dices of both. The other circles might represent what we have inherited from our friends, from the community, from the church and from the society in which we have lived. The outermost circles might stand for the way we have been influenced by being children of a particular country, of Mother Earth and of the universe.

We have been deeply influenced for the good by this environment. We have been aided by the universe, for example, in the realisation of our dream. This is an indebtedness we need to acknowledge. We may need to acknowledge and be grateful for the fact that much in our physical make-up has its origins in the fifteen-billion-year story of the universe. The story of its evolution is the story of how providence has moulded our humanity.

The environment: a second womb

Each of these circles, which represents our environment, has a certain similarity to the womb (the matrix) within which we spend our first nine months of life. Each is what we might call a second womb (the patrix) which forms and sustains us for the rest of our lives. The society in which we grow up shapes our mind and heart, our vision and values. Society challenges us to see the wisdom contained in our individual story in the light of the wisdom contained in its story. It challenges us to weigh the wisdom of our vision against the traditional wisdom it has accumulated over many generations. This traditional wisdom, embedded in the culture of the society in which we live, has a formative role to play in the way we think and in the way we feel. So there is a wisdom in our environment that seeks to expand and clarify our wisdom.

As in other areas of life, we tend to be a lot more conscious of the 10% of our environment that is negative than of the 90% that is positive. The black spot is always inclined to hold our attention and colour our attitudes, even though it is very far from being the whole picture. We need to redress this imbalance and learn to focus a lot more on society's constructive contribution to our lives.

Like Tom Wingo, we need to acknowledge and be grateful for all that is positive in the environment in which we have grown up. There is something disturbing about our being unaware of and ungrateful for all the gifts we have inherited from our environment. It has a generative role in making us, which is comparable to that of our family. It is through our environment that a large part of Providence's plan to realise our dream is realised.

Why have we lost touch with our environment?

At the beginning of the book of Genesis there is a picture of the intimate relationship God established between us and our environment. We were made partners with God in his work of creation and we were to care for it, while it in turn was meant to nourish us. This mutual concern disintegrated as a result of the Fall. Our close relationship with our environment fell apart and we became estranged from each other. Our surroundings, as a result, became hostile and we had to extract a livelihood from them.

> And to the man he said, 'Because you have listened to the voice of your wife, and have eaten of the tree about which I commanded you, "You shall not eat of it," cursed is the ground because of you; in toil you shall eat of it all the days of your life; thorns and thistles it shall bring forth for you; and you shall eat the plants of the field. By the sweat of your face you shall eat bread until you return to the ground, for out of it you were taken; you are dust, and to dust you shall return.' (Gen 3:17-19)

In our time, science and economics have contributed to our estrangement from our environment. The growth of science has led to much of our environment losing its significance and its deepest purpose. This was because science saw the world as the isolated parts of a great machine. As a result, the sense of everything in the world being a living organism, and thus interrelated and interdependent, was lost. Under the influence of science's view of all of creation as parts of a machine, providence became more and more remote. God was required only to create the machine and to set it in motion.

Even before the industrial revolution, people had ceased to see the world in terms of God's providence and has thus ceased to ask the question, 'Is it the will of God?' They had become more concerned with the pragmatic questions, 'Does it work?' and 'Does it pay?' The environment came to be seen in commercial terms. Greed edged out our grail quest and a consciousness of the role of the environment in the realisation of our dream was lost. Much of creation came to be seen merely as a source of raw material that could be exploited at will. This attitude is having disastrous effects on areas of our environment such as the rain forests of Brazil.

Building a better relationship

In this century, science has begun to re-discover the interrelatedness and interdependence of all the parts of our environment. There is a growing consciousness of our need to respect, and take responsibility for, our deep relationship with what forms for us our second womb. So in this exercise we are concerned to build a deeper relationship with our environment. This is what we might call 'a sympathetic one' in which we strive to befriend all those areas of our environment from which we have become estranged.

THE EXERCISE

1) We have been using a number of names for the world in which we live, such as, the environment, society, community, creation, the second womb and the universe. Notice which of these appeals to you most and then say what it means for you. Describe some key events in the growth of your awareness of your environment over the years. Have these experiences changed the way you see your environment?

2) Write down some of the ways you have benefited from your environment. Underline the ones that are more important so that you get a sense of their order of priority for you. Take one of these gifts of the environment that you value highly and consider what it would feel like if you had to do without it. Allow yourself time to let a sense of wonder before this aspect of your environment grow and be expressed.

3) List some aspects of the society in which you live which have the nature of a gift. Are these saying something to you about God's providence in your life? Take one of these gifts and write down what is being said to you by means of it.

4) Note some of the aspects of your environment that disturb you, for example, the ways your environment is abused. List some environmental issues that you feel strongly about. Describe one of these and say why you feel so strongly about it. If you had the power and the resources, what plan would you draw up to improve the environment in which you live?

5) Imagine yourself sharing what you have experienced in 4) with someone who is concerned about environmental issues. Let this person ask you what you think and how you feel about the environment. After having said all you want to, ask this person how

they feel about the environment and about your concern for it. Try to accept their acceptance and tolerance of your neglect of, or indifference to, aspects of your environment. See do they appreciate the good aspects of what for you may be a depressing picture of the way Mother earth is abused today.

6) List some of the areas of your environment that you feel very positively about. See what you appreciate most about these. Be with a wisdom figure and listen to what he or she thinks and feels concerning what is most important for you about the environment. Write down what this person says to you, and your own reactions to this.

7) You may now be in a position to enter a dialogue with some aspects of your environment. It may help you to get started if you recall some important events in the story of your relationship with your environment. Then make a focusing statement about where you stand at present. Let an important feature of your environment speak to you and then after listening, respond honestly to what it has to say to you. Continue until both of you have said all you want to. Write down the dialogue in outline or in full.

8) This part of the exercise is a fantasy in which you imagine the environment in which you have grown up to be like a second womb, a mother (*matrix*) or a father (*patrix*). Imagine the different parts of your environment as so many ways you are cared for, as by a parent, who has given you life and now sustains it. Next picture this atmosphere in which you live to be an expression of the way God cares for you and sustains your life. Let each part of the environment that forms this second womb reveal to you how it is a sacrament of God's love and providence. Respond to this as you go along, expressing how you feel.

Nature as a wayside sacrament

Flower in the crannied wall
I pluck you out of the crannies
I hold you here, root and all, in my hand
Little flower – but if I could understand
What you are, root and all, and all in all
I should know what God and man is.
(Tennyson)

There are two ways of looking at nature. One of these, views it as a necessary part of the environment that sustains us, not just materially but our spirit too. The other view is that nature has merely a functional value, for example, as a source of raw materials for making things. This latter view is dominant today and its destructiveness can be gauged from the following quotation.

Our culture takes pride in being scientific; our time is referred to as the Scientific Age. It is dominated by rational thought, and scientific knowledge is often considered the only acceptable kind of knowledge. That there can be intuitive knowledge or awareness which is just as valid and reliable, is generally not recognised. This attitude, known as scientism is widespread, pervading our educational system and all other social and political institutions.

Retreating into our minds, we have forgotten how to 'think' with our bodies, how to use them as agents of knowing. In doing so we have also cut ourselves off from our natural environment and have forgotten how to commune and cooperate with its rich variety of living organisms.

With the rise of Newtonian physics, finally, nature became a mechanical system that could be manipulated and exploited.

In our civilisation, we have modified our environment to such an extent during our cultural evolution, that we have lost touch with our biological and ecological base more than any other culture and any other civilisation in the past. This separation manifests itself in a striking disparity between the development of intellectual power, scientific knowledge, and technological skills on the one hand, and of wisdom, spirituality and ethics on the other.

Our progress, then, has been largely a rational and intellectual affair, and this one-sided evolution has now reached a highly alarming stage, a situation so paradoxical that it borders on insanity. (*The Turning Point* by Fritjof Capra)

The distorted vision

Nature is an important part of our environment. As such, it is part of that second womb' in which we are moulded and made, nurtured and sustained. What prevents this from happening, and defeats nature's whole purpose, is the mentality expressed in the Great Warrior Myth. As we saw already, this mentality breeds a lack of sensitivity and concern for many areas of life, including nature. As a result, we have the abuse or the destruction of nature. This takes many forms, for example, the pollution of air and water, the destruction of the rain forests, and the erosion of fertile soil . All this destruction takes place in the name of greed, respectfully masquerading as development or economic growth. The mentality bred by a myth like that of the Great Warrior, is at best indifferent to nature and at worst mindlessly destructive of it. When I look up a dictionary of modern quotations, I am struck by the way this negative mentality towards nature is reflected by quotations such as the following:

The whole of nature is a conjugation of the verb to eat, in the active and the passive. (W. R. Inge)

A vacuum is a hell of a lot better than some of the stuff that nature replaces it with. (Tennesee Williams)

In our indifference to, or even hostile attitude towards nature, we get cut off from something that is an essential part of us and we are impoverished as a result.

In the plan of creation, God establishes us as his co-creators. We are to be 'masters of ... all living creatures', responsible for looking after what God had made as good. We are to care for nature, and it in turn will nourish us.

Once we separate ourselves from God, we exclude ourselves from the garden of Eden. God is the centre of all creation, and once that centre no longer holds us together, things fall apart. As described in the story of the Fall, there is a breakdown of the original relationship which God established between all things. We get out of touch with God, ourselves, others and the whole of creation. Nature is no longer an object of our concern that in turn nourishes us. It becomes a hostile place.

> Accursed is the soil because of you. Painfully will you get your bread from it as long as you live. It will yield you brambles and thistles, as you eat the produce of the land. By the sweat of you face will you earn your food. (Gen 3:17-19)

The true vision

God is seeking to restore intimacy with us, to establish a covenant in which we will all 'know' him. (Jer 31:34) An essential feature of this covenant is that our lost intimacy and harmony with nature should be restored. This is the vision that Isaiah inspired. He foresees a state of harmony being reestablished between ourselves and nature when 'the whole earth is filled with the knowledge of God'. (Is 11: 6-9) To bring this dream to be, we have to co-operate in this work of reconciliation. This means that we have to befriend that part of God's creation, called nature, from which we have become estranged.

In his poem, *God's Grandeur*, Hopkins laments the fact that 'all is seared with trade; bleared, smeared with toil'. He is also hopeful, believing in nature's resilience and in its abiding power to display God's grandeur. His belief is that God is at work, seeking to restore a lost intimacy between ourselves and nature.

> The world is charged with the grandeur of God.
> It will flame out, like shining from shook foil;
> It gathers to a greatness, like the ooze of oil
> Crushed. Why do men then now not reck his rod?
> Generations have trod, have trod, have trod;
> And all is seared with trade; bleared, smeared with toil;
> And wears man's smudge and shares man's smell: the soil
> Is bare now, nor can foot feel, being shod.
> And for all this, nature is never spent;
> There lives the dearest freshness deep down things;

And though the last lights off the black West went
Oh, morning at the brown brink eastward, springs –
Because the Holy Spirit over the bent
World broods with warm breast and with ah! bright wings.

In this poem of Hopkins, hope is expressed for a freedom from the limiting and destructive effects of the Fall. There is also hope for a freedom for something new, which is the emergence again of our deep dream. Nature has a great power to facilitate both these kinds of freedom, to provide us with solitude and to put us in touch with our deep dream. Nature can become that part of our environment where we find space to be alone with ourselves, with another and with God. It is the quiet or desert place which Jesus invites us into when he says,

> Come apart to a quiet place by yourselves and rest for a little while. (Mk 6:31)

This invitation echoes the words of the prophet Hosea through which God expresses his desire to lead us into the quiet and solitude of the desert in order to speak to our depths.

> I will lure her and bring her into the wilderness and speak tenderly to her. (Hos 2:14)

Most people warm to the idea of nature as a means of getting away from it all. It is a place apart, an area of solitude, that is not subject to the pressures of the marketplace where:

> The world is too much with us; late and soon
> Getting and spending we lay waste our powers
> Little we see in Nature that is ours.
> (Wordsworth)

In nature, then, we can be put in touch again with our deepest selves and thus with God. It will, however, take a lot of effort to re-establish nature as a wayside sacrament, to find tongues in trees and good in everything.

> And this our life exempt from public haunt,
> Finds tongues in trees, books in the running brooks,
> Sermons in stones, and good in everything.
> (Shakespeare)

THE EXERCISE

1) Write briefly about the place that nature has in your life at present. Note the various steps in the story of the development of your present attitude. Are there images of nature that you warm to? What do these images say about the way you see and feel about nature now? Would you like your attitude to it to be different from what it is?

2) List some of the ways nature has been useful to you in your life and underline the more important ones. Pick out a few of nature's contributions to your well-being that you value most and describe the ways you are helped by these aspects of nature. Re-live an uplifting experience you had of nature and then notice how you feel about nature as a result. Contemplate the aspect of nature you have found uplifting and let a sense of wonder grow. You may want to express how you feel with a prayer of praise and gratitude such as Psalm 8.

3) Write down some aspects of nature about which you feel positively. After noticing and trying to articulate how you see and feel about one of these, share this with yourself, with a wisdom figure or with God.

4) Are there parts of nature that you react to in a negative way or with indifference? After you have noticed and named these, you might share how you feel about them with yourself, with a wisdom figure or with God.

5) Take one aspect of nature that means a lot to you and listen to what it has to say. It may reveal the goodness God found in it when he created it and found delight in what he had created. It may speak about the way it is God's gift to you and a wayside sacrament of his love, his presence and his providence. It may speak about how it is abused and the way you might remedy this.

6) Enter into a dialogue with nature by recalling some key points in the story of your relationship. You might both like to speak first about what your overall feeling for each other is, and then about more specific ways your lives intermingle. Write down what both of you say, in outline or in full.

7) A fantasy might help you to move into a more intimate relationship with nature. Imagine you are somewhere you like to enjoy nature and become attuned to the atmosphere of the place. Let

FOLLOW YOUR DREAM

God join you and ask you how you feel about some gift of nature. After saying how you feel about it, ask God what he intends it to mean for you. For example, God may open up the wonder of it for you and also what he intended in giving this gift to you.

The gift of technology

Technology has the power to foster our dream as well as to frustrate it. This was brought home to me recently by a film which highlighted the conflict of interests there are within the field of technology. There is, on the one hand, our natural desire to put technology at the service of human development. On the other hand, so much of technology is at the disposal of economic growth which has other ideas for the use of technology than the betterment of our human lot. I would like to start with the story of the film.

Lorenzo's Oil is about a young boy who was suffering from a disease called ALD. This meant that he had only two years to live and that the lead-up to his death would be very painful. His parents refused to accept the fact that their child must die. They listened to what the doctors and the scientists had to say and struggled to carry on from where they left off. Lorenzo's mother devoted herself tirelessly to nursing her child while his father began to systematically research every aspect of his son's disease.

The scientists they consulted seemed to centre on their own process of investigation and on their need to be objective and not to get too caught up in the human situation. They felt they had to retain a certain detachment if they were to solve what for them was a scientific problem. They could not afford to be drawn off course by getting too involved in the heart-breaking situation of parents such as Lorenzo's. Some of the other parents of ALD sufferers formed an organisation to support one another and to cooperate with doctors and scientists in their search for a solution. Their role was to wait and to put their trust in the scientists and to leave it to them to find a solution in their own time. It was as if these parents were small circles of concern within the vast circle of science and the almost magical power it held out as their only hope.

If Lorenzo's parents had been willing to wait for science to come up with a cure for ALD, their son would have died. But at the centre of their world was the life of their child and they used all that science and technology had to offer to secure their child's life. Eventually they were able to draw a number of scientists, doctors and even business people into the circle of providence they formed around this very sick child. As a result they found a remedy and their child is still alive. The film ends with a series of shots of different children who suffered from ALD. They had recovered from their illness and were enjoying a normal life thanks to the concern of Lorenzo's parents.

This story epitomises the power of technology when it is at the service of concern for human life. As became clear in the film, this was not the normal concern of technology which is usually at the service of science's effort to solve problems and economics' effort to make a profit. In the film we have an example of a world which was dominated by the concern for human life and where everything was at the service of this providence-like concern.

It is as if there were two spheres of influence at work in the story. One sphere was dominated by science, economics and technology. This sphere was willing to take in other concerns in a subordinate role as long as these did not interfere with its own interests. The other sphere was dominated by the parents of Lorenzo and their all pervading concern for human life. In this latter sphere, science and technology had an indispensable and most creative role to play.

The creative use of technology

The creative genius of technology is undoubted. It has provided us with such wonders as radio, television, electricity and the telephone. These have improved our standard of living in a remarkable way. When we compare the time and the hardship involved in a long journey a hundred years ago, it is hard to doubt the benefits which technology has brought in the form of modern means of transport.

The benefits of technology might be summed up in its unique power to extend the horizons of our understanding and concern.

It can put us in touch with a much wider world and it provides us with the facilities to take responsibility for bettering that world. An example of how it can foster the concern, which is central to our dream, is the way that the skilful use of television made the world aware of the desperate effects of famine in Ethiopia. In response there was a wave of compassion and all the technical expertise involved in Band Aid's efforts to organise relief supplies. So technology has a unique power to keep us in touch with a wider world and its problems, as well as making it possible to do something about these.

Broadening our horizons
Technology opens up immense possibilities for dealing with the problems it makes us aware of. If the money and expertise that are at present at the disposal of the production of arms, were put towards solving problems, such as that of world hunger, the practical sympathy of the Good Samaritan would find a new face in technology.

Our expertise in this field could also be put to use in the whole area of justice, where our concern is to provide an environment not just were people can get by. Justice requires the provision of the kind of conditions where people can develop their full potential. We have always associated technology with outer space rather then with our inner journey, with the aggressive promotion of our ego world than with that of our essence. We have here an issue of basic justice, for technology must help us to follow our dream as well as provide for our material needs.

The abuse of technology
Technology is a gift of God and it can be a powerful aid towards realising our dream. We have to face the fact that it has also the potential to become a modern tower of babel.

The Tower of Babel
In the book of Genesis, at the end of the description of the effects of the Fall, we have the story of the Tower of Babel. In the story, people became conscious of the disintegrating effect of having separated themselves from God. Having forfeited the true source of their happiness, they burden the material world with providing a happiness for them which it was not designed to provide. They say to themselves, 'Come, let us

build ourselves a tower with its top reaching to heaven. Let us make a name for ourselves and hold together, lest we be scattered all over the earth.' The effect of building the tower to get happiness by their own resources is disastrous. Deprived of the centre for which they were made, the God who held them together, they disintegrate and are scattered throughout the world. This is symbolised in the story by their language becoming confused 'so that they no longer understood one another'.

What is symbolised by this story is the end result of people separating themselves from God. They then rely on the material world to fill the void left by the absence of the God from whom they have separated themselves. This is a weight that technology was not meant to bear. It was meant be an aid to realising our dream and not to provide a substitute for it.

The following are some extracts from a modern description of the abuse of technology symbolised by the Babel story:

> More than fifteen million people – most of them children – die of starvation each year; another 500 million are seriously undernourished. Almost 40% of the world's population has no access to professional health services; yet developing countries spend more than three times as much on armaments as on health care. 35% of humanity lacks safe drinking water, while half of its scientists and engineers are engaged in the technology of making arms… Nuclear weapons do not increase our security, as the military establishment would have us believe, but merely increase the likelihood of global destruction.

> It has become clear that our technology is severely disturbing, and may even be destroying, the ecological systems upon which our very existence depends.

> Our science and technology are based on the seventeenth century belief that an understanding of nature implies domination of nature by 'man' … This attitude has produced a technology that is unhealthy and inhuman; a technology in which the natural, organic habitat of complex human beings is replaced by a simplified, synthetic, and prefabricated environment. (Capra, *The Turning Point*)

A technology 'unhealthy and inhuman'
The abuse of technology is seen by Capra to arise from an overem-

phasis of the *yang* element in our culture to the near exclusion of the *yin* element. These, as we saw in Exercise 24, are Chinese terms that correspond roughly with what we would identify as the *male* and the *female* aspects of our lives. Both these elements are good and remain healthy as long as a proper balance is kept between the two. Either can become destructive when there is an imbalance.

An example of this imbalance of the yang and yin in our times is the arms industry. In it is employed a huge percentage of our technical expertise and on it is spent over 1 billion dollars every day. All this on something that is so destructive. Alongside this we have, according to a UN report, 1 billion people living in 'absolute poverty', their lives 'so characterised by malnutrition, illiteracy and disease as to be beneath any reasonable definition of human dignity'. This is a terrible abuse of the gift of technology.

Bryan Appleyard in his book, *Understanding the Present*, expresses the belief that even though science is a distinctly human creation, its priorities are not humans and their cares. It has replaced a benevolent providence with a detached quest for knowledge that is characteristic of our society's exclusive preference for the yang. As we saw in the story of *Lorenzo's Oil*, science and technology are good servants of providence but a poor substitute. The poet Petrarch, before the new knowledge was given the name science, saw that its main concern was not the care of us human beings and 'whence we came and whither we go'.

> Even if these things were true, they help in no way towards a happy life, for what does it advantage us to be familiar with the nature of animals, birds, fishes and reptiles, while we are ignorant of the race of man to which we belong, and do not care whence we came and whither we go.

Technology is the child of two very powerful parents, science and economics. Once we take technology into our homes, its parents will come along as well. Appleyard believes that the overall influence of this combination is that many of our problems will be solved and there will be many benefits. This is why technology is so seductive. We need, however, to be aware of the tendency of science, economics and technology to become a substitute for providence. In the sixteenth century, science modestly asserted that there were only a limited number of questions it felt competent to answer. In our time science has arrogantly asserted that its questions are the only valid ones. It has become the arbiter of what is real and significant. Rather than nourish our dream, it is inclined to dominate, diminish and distort it, because of its lack of concern for what gives our lives meaning and purpose.

The story about the Dream Merchant, in Chapter 1, is highly relevant here. Rather than technology broadening our horizons, it narrows the limits of who and what we are sensitive to and concerned about to our superficial dream. We become alienated from more and more of our world and out of touch with the real human priorities.

At the service of our deep dream

Since the industrial revolution, technology has been so much in the service of greed that it is hard for it to speak its truth. This truth as we have seen in the story of *Lorenzo's Oil* is to be found, not in the Great Warrior myth but in that of the Good Samaritan. Because the true role of technology has been so obscured, we will find it hard to appreciate as realistic the fact that technology's true purpose is to promote our dream. In order that technology might reveal its true purpose, we have to give it a voice by becoming aware of its true nature. Technology, like all else in creation, wants to reveal itself to us, so that we might come to know and value its dream, as well as its role in realising ours.

If we take as an example a piece of technology like a film, we may see how it can be used to put us in touch with our deep dream. There is no doubt that many films reflect the masculine imbalance in our culture. They reflect its violence and its tendency to escape from our dream into the trivial. There is, however, a growing sensitivity to the deeper or more spiritual side of us evident in many films today. With its skilled use of symbols that speak to us today, cinema has a unique power to help us satisfy our grail hunger. I was struck by the truth of this recently when a reflective young man said to me that he got his main religious experience at films. Television too has tremendous power to influence us in its skilful use of symbols. Very often, however, its agenda is aimed much more at stimulating our superficial dream than at awakening our deep dream.

For too long, technology has been at the service of the yang or male side of our culture. It needs now to reach a balance by being put much more at the service of human relations, at the service of intimacy and harmony with ourselves, with God and with others, at the service of our dream.

THE EXERCISE

1) Write down some of the kinds of technology that you find helpful and say how you feel about these. Has your attitude to technology changed over the years? Are there kinds of technology that used to cause you wonder and that you now take for granted? What images and feelings do you associate with the way technical things affect your lifestyle?

2) What kinds of technology do you appreciate most as having improved your life? Select one that you value highly and imagine what life would be like without it. Note what difference its absence would make to your life. Take one kind of technology that is important for you and allow yourself to move beyond its functional value to wonder at its ingenuity, or at some awe inspiring quality it has. Be with the words that are repeated in the book of Genesis, 'God saw that what he had created was good' and let yourself be with God's delight in what caused you wonder.

3) Reflect on whether you see the piece of technology you have been focusing on as a gift of God, or does it lack that dimension for you? Spend time letting the sense of it being a gift sink in. You may notice that you have been taking the fact that it is a gift for granted.

Consider for a while the fact that people who give you gifts are giving you signs, they are saying that they have thought of you and want to show you that they care. Spend time with the reality that the piece of technology you are considering is a gift of God, and note how it is expressing something of God's love and providence in your life. Record how you react to this reality. Does it seem a bit unreal or is it exciting? Would you like your response to be different?

4) Sketch out some of your reflections on the way technology has adversely affected your way of life. Do its negative qualities form a large part of your picture of it? Do these, like a black spot on a sheet of paper, fix your attention? Have you, as a result, a prejudiced view of technology? Describe one area of technology which

makes you feel uneasy and then note the negative feelings it arouses in you. Share these feelings with the part of yourself which admires technology.

5) Dwell on and note down the positive aspects of technology. Allow yourself time to appreciate the constructive role it plays in your life. This is an effort to get freedom from the way the black spot, symbolising the negative aspects of technology, can dominate your attention. So concentrate on the way technology has opened up new possibilities for you, and on how it promises to do so more and more in the future.

To get a truer picture of the immense contribution of technology to life, it might help to draw a diagram. In it, highlight the kinds of technology that most enrich your life.

6) From your experiences of the exercise so far, could you form a symbol of 'who' technology is for you? For example, he, she or it may be like a facilitator helping you to communicate better with other people. So, let technology assume this personal role and then listen to what it has to say.

7) After quietening and centring yourself, enter a dialogue with technology. Start by outlining how you now feel about this aspect of your life, and then let it reply. Continue until each of you have said all you want to about how you see and feel about each other. When you have finished, read back through the dialogue and notice how you both feel about your relationship.

8) Allow yourself time to become quiet and then enter your inner room where you can speak to God in this very personal atmosphere. (Mt 6:6) Around the walls of this inner room, notice the way your story is recorded in a variety of images such as photographs and symbols. Notice in particular the images which speak of the place technology has played in your story. Let God join you and be enthusiastic about all of this. Then allow God to lead you to the tapestry of your life which has a central place in your inner room. Together you look at the way technology has added a special dimension to this tapestry, through, for example, allowing you to travel, to listen to the best of music and to be in touch with a wider world. Allow yourself time to appreciate all of this and then respond honestly to it.

PART V

Introduction to Exercises 29-30

Letting our lives be shaped by our dream
So far in these exercises we have been seeking to discover, explore and own our dream. It is vital that we now take what we have been doing a step further. We must take responsibility for letting our dream shape the way we live our lives.

Finding the Lion in the Stone
When the little boy asked the sculptor how he knew the magnificent lion he had carved was in the stone, he eventually got the answer, 'I had to find the lion in my heart before I could find it in the stone!'

Even though the sculptor had to find it in his heart first, he was not happy just to leave it there. It had to be given concrete expression, and that had to be in harmony with what was in his heart. Giving it concrete expression is no easy task, for the sculptor must wrestle with the stone until what he chisels out of it is in keeping with what he has found in his heart.

We have seen how *we* have to find the lion in *our* hearts in the discovery, the exploration and the appropriation of our deep dream. It now remains for us to integrate our dream, to make sure that it is given expression in our decisions and in the way we act. We will thus give our dream it's full expression. This is the main work of art God commissions us with in life.

The law of consistency
We naturally feel a need to make sure the expression we give our dream is consistent with the dream itself. This consistency is demanded by our very make-up, more than by outside influences. On this law, written on our hearts, rests the call of Christ, not only to listen to the word but also to find an appropriate expression of it in the way we live.

Why do you call me 'Lord, Lord', and not do what I tell you? Every one who comes to me and hears my words and does them, I will show you what he is like; he is like a man building a house, who dug deep and laid the foundations upon rock; and when the flood arose, the stream broke against that house and could not shake it, because it had been well built. But he who hears and does not do them is like a man who built a house on the ground without a foundation; against which the stream broke, and immediately it fell, and the ruin of that house was great. (Lk 6:46-49)

We have a sense, like that of an artist, that will tell us when the expression we are giving our dream is just right. This sense is what we call conscience and we know when our conscience is at ease and content and when it is not.

Exercise 29 will deal with the way our *desires* are an indication of what areas of our dream we are ready to implement.

Exercise 30 will deal with the call to make the *decisions* which are necessary to implement our dream or give it expression in the way we live.

Desire as your guiding star

'Desire is the guiding star of the outlaw.' This striking statement is from a book called *The Passionate Life* by Sam Keen. In it he expresses his belief that all through life there is a healthy outlaw in us, whom we must respect and listen to. So as well as the voice of tradition, by which we must be guided, there is this other voice. It calls for obedience to the unique person each of us is, to our individual aspirations and to our deep personal desires.

Deep within you is written your own song.
Sing it with all your heart.

Like the dream in the acorn, ours never rests in its search for maturity. At times, the energy behind this dream may appear to be inactive. It will, however, keep surging up from our unconscious like the burst of new life that transforms a tree in Spring. This energy, inherent in our dream, surfaces as desire. So our deep desires are a manifestation of our grail quest, the onward movement of our dream seeking fulfilment.

Why we do not listen to our desires

These deep desires that manifest our deep dream's thirst for fulfilment make big claims on our time and energy. They, therefore, stir up a lot of resistance. For this reason we may welcome the offer of the Dream Merchant whom we met in Chapter 1. We may feel that the desires which spring from our dream are too demanding and too difficult for us to entertain. So, selling our soul's deep dream to the Dream Merchant is a much more subtle temptation than it may at first appear.

There is a great danger that we allow our deep dream and its desires to be drowned out by those of our superficial dream. In the parable of the Sower, Jesus illustrates how easily the word, and the spiritual desires it generates, is smothered or drowned out by the demands of other voices.

And as for what fell among the thorns, they are those who hear, but as they go on their way they are choked by the cares and riches and pleasures of life, and their fruit does not mature. (Lk 8:14)

The change desire calls for

The Crab's Shell
There is a certain kind of crab that lives in a shell but not the one shell for life. As it grows, it must discard the old shell that it has outgrown or it will die. Changing shells is not as easy as removing one's overcoat, for the shell has to be split open and then it must be very vulnerable until a new shell has grown. When the crab's shell becomes too thick, too tough to crack open, the crab cannot grow any more. That is when it dies.

One of the greatest threats to the realisation of our dream is that we settle for meeting expectations, our own and those of others. By thus living in a world of 'oughts' we lose touch with what we really want, with the deep desires which spring from our dream. To be indifferent to our deep desires means that we become inflexible and refuse to grow. We become like the crab which dies because it is no longer able to break open the shell it has outgrown.

For someone brought up as I was, adjusting to this way of being led by God is not easy. My mind keeps returning to guidance being found through discovering the very clear-cut 'will of God'. This was always somewhere outside, and over against, my own field of personal experience. The concept of the will of God can easily be understood in terms of expectations. It is associated with things we ought to do and with an outer authority. It is not associated much with the inner authority of the 'still small voice' of the Spirit inspiring us with desire. This inner authority of people's personal experience appears a lot more vague, intangible and open to error than does the clear concreteness of what most people understand by the will of God.

Remaining in touch with our desires
The desires inspired by our dream never leave us. They may be drowned out by the voice of our own or other people's expectations and by the aggressiveness of our superficial dream. They may become dormant, but they never abandon us. As they are in-

built they will, no matter how we repress them, keep surging up and moving us onward to that fullness of life which is Jesus' dream for us.

> I have come that you may have life and have it in abundance. (Jn 10:10)

What is this fullness of life we are urged on towards by means of our desires? Each of us has to discover and take responsibility for the answer we give to this question. Here, however, we will assume, that in general terms the life Jesus offers us what satisfies our essential hunger. This is a hunger which only God can satisfy and it is one he plans to satisfy by revealing himself to us. So our basic desires come out of a hunger that *we are*. 'You have made us for yourself O Lord ...'

In his letter to the Ephesians, Paul describes how God plans to satisfy our essential hunger by filling us with himself. (Eph 3 19) God wants to share with us not just all he possesses but his whole person by self disclosure. Paul understands that this will be realised through our being led, step by step, into the length and breadth, the height and depth of the love God discloses himself to be.

> For this reason I bow my knees before the Father, from whom every family in heaven and on earth is named, that according to the riches of his glory he may grant you to be strengthened with might through his Spirit in the inner man, and that Christ may dwell in your hearts through faith; that you, being rooted and grounded in love, may have power to comprehend with all the saints what is the breadth and length, the height and depth, and to know the love of Christ which surpasses knowledge, that you may be filled with all the fullness of God. (Eph 3:14-19)

As we have emphasised in Exercises 2, 8 and 16 especially, it is fundamental to our understanding of our deep desires that it is the Spirit who inspires them. Our role is to be receptive and to listen. If we are receptive, the Spirit will guide us, bit by bit, to realise the potential of the love which has been planted in our hearts. (Rom 5:5) The bit we are ripe to realise at any particular point in our life can be best discerned by keeping in touch with our desires. These desires will tell us, not only where we are ready to move, but when the time is ripe for this.

Staying tuned to our desires

God will all the time be building up our desire to realise those areas of our dream for which we are ripe. Our desires will therefore vary in their insistence according as we are ripe to realise them or not. As a result, we need to be constantly discerning the intensity of our desires. The alternative is that we either remain insensitive to where growth is called for or that we may run ahead of God. Running ahead of God means that we do not allow ourselves enough time to discern our desires before we act on them. The mere emergence of a certain desire may make us feel that God wants us to act on it long before we have sufficient clarity and energy to do so. This temptation may be born of an image of God as demanding.

Quite the contrary, God according to the prophet Jeremiah is one who 'seduces' us ('wins us by attractiveness' according to the dictionary). The God who leads us by inspiring deep desires, works on, what a teacher I once had, used to call, the principle of the honey pot. He explained what he meant by saying that if you want to move a bear around, you do not start pushing it. Instead, you work on the principle of attraction. In the belief that bears love honey, you attach a pot of honey to a long stick. Then when you have brought the honey to the attention of the bear, you can lead it wherever you wish.

> He calls his own sheep by name and leads them out. When he has brought out all his own, he goes before them, and the sheep follow him, for they know his voice. (Jn 10:3-4)

THE EXERCISE

1) It would be interesting first of all to make some notes on what comes to mind when you imagine what the fullness of your deep dream would be like. This would involve, for example, trying to describe what, in your view, it would mean to enjoy a very full and happy life. When you compare what you have written with Jesus' statement, that he has come that you may have the fullness of life (Jn 10:10), what is your reaction? Write out what in practical terms is your ideal in life.

2) If you were to imagine yourself with no restrictions of time and energy, what way would you arrange your life in order to live it to the full. List your desires as spontaneously as you can, with no re-

strictions as to what you are going to do about them or what is feasible. Your list should cover all aspects of your ideal of living life to the full.

3) Make a list of what you feel would be the more basic needs for 'having life in abundance'. As a way of becoming more aware of the relative importance of your basic needs, you may find it helpful to draw a diagram. The more important needs might be put in an inner circle and less significant ones in other circles further removed from the centre.

4) List the desires that are more pressing at this stage of your life. Distinguish those desires which are deeper from the more superficial ones. Is there an order of priority you would establish among the deeper desires? A diagram similar to that in 3) may help you clarify the relative importance of the desires in your life right now.

5) Note down the kinds of resistance you notice to your deep desires. What prevents your realising them? What kind of superficial desires do you find most insistent? What ways do you notice these smothering your deeper ones?

6) Enter a fantasy in which you imagine yourself in a quiet place. When you have quietened yourself, let Jesus join you. He asks you what you want out of life now. Let him talk to you about what you want, and then let yourself respond honestly to what he says. Jesus next speaks to you about his wish to help you to fulfil your deep desires and how he will be guiding you towards this. In the light of Jn 1:39, be with the reality of his wanting for you what you most deeply desire. Note down your reaction to this and to other areas of the fantasy which moved you.

7) Write some of the main memories in the story of one of your deep desires and then say how you see and feel about it now. Next begin a dialogue with this part of yourself that has this deep desire and write down what each of you have to say to each other.

8) At times in your life you took a road that meant you closed off the possibilities of taking other ones. You may, for example, have been too busy to keep up with a certain friend and thereby lost touch with him or her. This may be an experience worth going back to, so that you might wander down that road which you closed off. This would be a matter of opening up the possibilities

of that friendship and how it might have developed and the potential you might have realised in it.

9) Spend time making your way up a mountain to meet your wisdom figure. Savour all the things you enjoy about the ascent, especially the natural beauty of the scenery and the sense of freedom and perspective that your journey gives you. Your wisdom figure whom you journey to meet could be a person in history, a significant person in your own story or one of the persons of the Trinity. This person talks to you about your ideals and aspirations and especially about what is most important for you just now. When you are alone again, write down your reflections on this meeting and how you reacted to what was revealed to you in it.

The creative power of decision

We are in a sense our own parents and bring ourselves to birth by our decisions. (Gregory Nazianzen)

One of the features that we noticed about our dream in Chapter 1 is that it will not be realised without our decision. We saw that our dream is very different from the one in the acorn, where the dream is automatically realised. Unless something drastic happens, the dream in the acorn will realise itself in a fully grown oak tree. With us, however, unless we choose to become sensitive and responsive to our dream, it will not be realised.

God who made us without our consent, will not save us without our consent. (St Augustine)

We have a problem giving this consent and living consistently with our decision. This is largely because there are a lot of very tempting alternatives which demand much less effort and are more immediately rewarding.

The vital decision
A young man was walking along a road one day when he met someone who was carrying two bundles, one large and the other small. On being offered a choice between the two, the young man decided to go and consult the elders before making a decision. While he was away some other people came along the road and they were given the same choice. They were curious to know what each of the bundles contained and were told that the small one contained life and that the other contained many of the good things of life. They asked to see the contents of the large bundle and immediately on seeing these they chose them. Ever since it has been difficult for people to choose life.

This story symbolises the important decision we are called upon to make, not just from time to time, but in an ongoing way. We are constantly faced with the fork in the road and we have to choose between the way which leads to life and that which leads to death.

See, I have set before you this day life and good, death and evil. If you obey the commandments of the Lord your God ... by loving the Lord your God, by walking in his ways ... then you will live and multiply.

But if your heart turns away, and you will not hear, but are drawn away to worship other gods and serve them, I declare to you this day, that you shall perish, you will not live long in the land which you are entering ... I have set before you life and death, blessing and curse; therefore choose life that you and your descendants may live, loving the Lord your God, obeying his voice and clinging to him; for that means life to you and length of days. (Deut 30:15-20)

Jesus, in the following brief parable, heightens our awareness of how critical our decision is. This is because the road to life is 'narrow and hard' demanding as it does a very disciplined effort, if we are to realise our potential for growth. This disciplined effort is often compared to rowing against the flow of the river. The alternative of shipping our oars and drifting comes very easily to us and leads to what Jesus terms 'destruction'.

Enter by the narrow gate; for the gate is wide and the way is easy that leads to destruction, and those who enter by it are many. For the gate is narrow and the way is hard that leads to life, and those who find it are few. (Mt 7:13-14)

The vital decision

The word *decision* may call to mind the notion of choosing between two or more ways of acting in a particular situation. Many of our decisions may be such, but the kind of decision we are looking at in this exercise is a more basic one. It is a choice that is permanently facing us between two key visions of ourselves.

The two visions are symbolised for us by the story about Rapunzel that we had in Exercise 4. There, Rapunzel had to choose whether to believe the witch or the young man, and the choice made all the difference to her happiness. In the same way, what we choose to believe, whether a distorted vision of ourselves or that which we see in Christ's eyes, is going to determine whether we walk the road to life or to destruction. Which vision we should choose seems obvious, but in reality it is a very difficult choice to make and follow through with.

FOLLOW YOUR DREAM

The specific reason why the decision to believe the Good News is so difficult is that it involves replacing deeply ingrained prejudices with the true vision of ourselves that Jesus invites us to accept. This radical change of mind and heart is what Jesus calls *repentance*. It is the most crucial decision of our life as it is the precondition of our belief in the Good News. Thus, if we are to accept this basic Christian vocation to repent and believe the gospel, we will have to fulfil certain conditions.

The basic content of our decisions

The most concrete condition we need to fulfil is that of making space in our day for getting in touch with our dream and taking responsibility for its realisation. If we cannot find the time and the energy for this, nothing much will happen and we will easily drift down the road to destruction.

> For evil to triumph it is sufficient for good people to do nothing. (Edmund Burke)

The benefits of making this space range from the dramatic improvement of health that Dr H Benson describes in his book, *The Relaxation Response*, to the increase of life and happiness that time apart with God makes possible.

The main thing that we need to make space for is *prayer*. This is the key way that we can answer the basic call of Jesus to 'repent and believe the Good News'. As we have seen in Exercise 13, prayer is our response to God's self disclosure to us. It is crucial that we listen to God's revelation of himself. This is the condition of our coming to know God and of having the life he promises (Jn 17:3)

Through *reflection* we learn to discern the way we are affected by the two voices that influenced Rapunzel. We learn to recognise which of the voices is leading us and where we are being led, either along the road to 'life' or down the road to 'destruction'. One voice, that of the Spirit, leads us into the extent and depth of God's love by enlightening and attracting us. The other voice is that of all in and around us, which resists belief in God's love.

Where *reflection* discerns what is being revealed to us, *prayer* appropriates this revelation and overcomes all that resists it.

The decisions we must make

It is only very gradually that we can learn the skills of prayer and reflection as the key way of answering the essential call of Christ. Answering this call is a life's work to be accomplished step by step. It is important that we have some way of deciding what we should take on at any one time. The following three points about a decision may form a useful guideline:

1) Our decision must be primarily concerned with what is basic to answering our essential call to believe the gospel. We must make our decision centre on the response which God's revelation of himself to each person calls for. Therefore, the prayer and reflection which are central to this response should be a focal point for our decisions.

2) Since the only way we can change our minds and hearts is bit by bit, it is important that in our decisions we do not take on too much at any one time. Centring our decision on a basic minimum is very realistic. Otherwise we become overburdened by our resolutions and do not stick to them.

It is important to follow the old adage about not running ahead of God. Like any good teacher, God respects the saying that to teach a person who is not ripe, is a waste of words. The small amount or basic minimum we are ripe for will be made clear, as we saw in Exercise 29, by the build-up of the desires God inspires in us.

3) Our decision should focus on what we really want. We need to distinguish this from what we feel we ought to do, or from the expectations of others. To be ruled by what we expect of ourselves, or what others expect of us, is contrary to all that we saw in Exercise 29 about the way God leads us.

THE EXERCISE

1) Select from your list of desires in the previous exercise, a basic minimum you would now like to do something about. Remember that your objective is a small number of things that at present you really want. Write these out, being as specific as you can as to what you feel called to do. It may help to put this down spontaneously first of all and then to edit it.

2) Next, write down what exactly you want to do about each of the objectives you have set yourself. It may help you to outline some suggestions, as you would to someone you were advising. From these suggestions, select what is essential. It is very impor-

tant to be specific as to what you want to do. One of our favourite escapes from our responsibility is to leave things very general.

3) Come back to your plan of action a number of times, after you have finished it, and see how you feel about what you have planned to do. Notice if you feel at ease, or if you are not quite content with it. It is good to keep modifying your plan until it fits you like a well-made garment.

4) You are now in a position to implement what you have decided to do. It is as well to keep in mind how faltering our efforts can be in the face of our well-established ways of doing things. We need to be patient while new habits are developing. We have to allow ourselves to fail a number of times and not to be discouraged by our broken resolutions. Write a little about your past experience of making decisions that came to nothing. Notice what images and feelings this arouses. What is the most common cause of your failing to follow through on your decisions?

6) In your efforts to hold yourself to what you have decided to do, it will help if you can talk about how you are getting on, with someone who is sympathetic. To share your decisions with another will help you to clarify what you want to do. It will also help towards implementing them, if you are accountable to someone else for what you are doing about your decisions.

Describe what you find yourself at ease with in these suggestions and what you find yourself resisting.

7) Sometimes when your decision is a major one between two alternatives, the following procedure may help. Take an example of this kind of decision from your own experience and do this part of the exercise with that decision in mind.

Write down all the reasons for, and all those against, what you are proposing to do. Deal with the pros and the cons at separate times and underline the more weighty reasons on each side of the decision. This should help you to sort out the genuine reasons from the more emotional ones. These may be mixed up together and the emotional ones may appear very strong until you put them on paper. Finally, it is important to stay with each side of the decision separately over a period of some days, and to measure how content each side leaves you.

Life's Main Artwork

This book has been all about the dream which God has built into you. As we have seen, however, your dream will not be realised, in the way that God has planned, unless you become sensitive and responsive to it. You are invited to make the realisation of your dream your main work in life. If you accept this invitation you will, like an artist, have to get in touch with your dream and then to take responsibility for realising it.

The dream you have to get in touch with is inspired by the Spirit's gift of love which is planted like a seed in your heart. (Rom 5:5) In your efforts to discover, explore and make your own of this love, you will be constantly guided by the same Spirit. (Jn 16:13])

There will never be anything more momentous that you will be asked to do in life than the creation of this unique work of art. This bringing of the seed, which the Spirit has planted in you, to full flower, is the most creative thing you will ever do. It is your life's main artwork.

> Softer than dew. But where the morning wind
> Blows down the world, O Spirit! show Thy Power:
> Quicken the dreams within the languid mind
> And bring Thy seed to flower.
> (E Underhill)